200

COCKTAIL PARTY RECIPES

CAROL BECKERMAN

SELLERS
PUBLISHING

A Quintet Book

Published by Sellers Publishing, Inc.
161 John Roberts Road, South Portland, Maine 04106
Visit our Web site: www.sellerspublishing.com
E-mail: rsp@rsvp.com

ISBN: 978-1-4162-4561-2
Library of Congress Control Number: 2015930717
QTT.RFCP

This book was conceived, designed and produced by
Quintet Publishing Limited
4th Floor, Sheridan House
114-116 Western Road
Hove, East Sussex
BN3 1DD

Project Editor: Ella Lines
Photographer: Tony Briscoe
Food Stylist: Julia Azzarello
Designer: Rod Teasdale
Art Director: Michael Charles
Editorial Director: Emma Bastow
Publisher: Mark Searle

10 9 8 7 6 5 4 3 2 1

Printed in China by Toppan Leefung

CONTENTS

introduction

Cocktail parties are easy to plan, glamorous, relatively inexpensive, and usually of a reasonably short duration. They are mostly held during the cocktail hour, that magic time, just before dinner, when you can indulge your fancy for cocktails and innovative new flavors to excite your guests' taste buds. Cocktail party food is amazingly versatile, with contrasting colors and flavors, tempting your guests to indulge in a delicious mix of different appetizers and hors d'oeuvres. The key to any great party is for the host to have as much fun as the guests, and organization is the key to ensure a stress-free get-together.

In this book you will find all you need to plan and execute the best cocktail party that you can imagine, one that will have your guests talking about it long after they reluctantly drag themselves away. From canapés to delightful little pies and sweet treats, there will be plenty of ideas for you to choose from, to make sure you have the right balance of hot and cold food.

planning

Remember that cocktail parties are usually hosted before or after the dinner hour. The food is not meant to replace a meal. A good rule of thumb is three to five different types of hors d'oeuvres, with two to three of each per person. If you decide that your party should take place during meal hours, there should be enough food to replace the meal, which means six to ten types of hors d'oeuvres with two to three of each per person. Men tend to eat more than women, so if there are more men, plan a few more dishes. Balance the menu, and aim for a variety—meat, vegetarian, hot, cold, spicy, and sweet. Offer hot food alongside room temperature dips, and spicy food contrasting with simple sandwiches. Choose some food that you can prepare ahead of time so there is less to do on the day, and prepare at least one vegetarian offering.

Invitations are not necessary for informal gatherings, a simple telephone call or email several weeks in advance is fine. If it is a formal affair, invitations can be sent out three to four weeks in advance, or even earlier if the event is very important. Be sure to include an R.S.V.P., and do not hesitate to call people for responses, as not knowing how to calculate quantities for an event is difficult.

When calculating how many invitations to issue, be strict about the size that fits your space. The average-size room can generally accommodate 30 people, a three-room expansive space will fit about 60. For any form of buffet, you should provide some seating, at least one for every two guests. Consider renting equipment or even a place to hold your venue.

When planning your party, it is great to choose a theme. It can be very simple such as a flavor, or particular color that is present throughout the entire evening. Getting creative can make your party feel special without adding to the budget, and it will help inspire the menu and decorations.

Designate a friend or two to help hand out food, serve cocktails, and collect glasses, so that you have time to mingle with your guests.

part-baked & pre-baked pastry shells

Pastry shells are ideal for holding lots of different fillings, and you can buy them pre-baked or part-baked, or make your own using a 12-cup tartlet pan or individual tartlet shells. Choose tartlets that are about 2 ½ inches in diameter.

2 ¾ cups/12 oz. all-purpose flour

½ cup/4 oz. butter, cold from the fridge, and cubed, plus extra for greasing

¼ cup/2 oz. shortening, cold from the fridge, and cubed

¼ tsp. salt

Makes 24

Generously grease a 24-cup (2 ½-inch) tartlet pan or 24 individual tartlet shells with butter.

In a food processor, pulse the flour, butter, shortening, and salt together until it resembles coarse bread crumbs.

Add 5 tablespoons iced water, pulse, add another tablespoon and pulse again. Pulse until a dough comes together, adding a little extra water, if necessary. Turn the dough out onto a lightly floured worktop, and knead into a round. Roll out to just under ¼-inch thick, and cut out rounds with a 3-inch plain cutter.

Transfer the rounds to the greased 24-cup tartlet baking pan, and transfer it to the refrigerator for 30 minutes to chill.

Pre-heat the oven to 400°F. Remove the pan from the refrigerator and fill each of the pastry shells with a few baking beans. Bake for 10 minutes. Remove from the oven, and let cool in the pan for 5 minutes. Take out the baking beans and set aside to cool.

now try these

pre-baked pastry shells
Follow the basic recipe, but bake for 15 minutes, remove from the oven and leave in the pan to cool for 5 minutes. Take out the baking beans and transfer to a wire rack to cool.

sweet pre-baked pastry shells
If you are using the pastry shells for a sweet filling, follow the basic recipe, but just before adding the water, add 2 tablespoons sugar to the food processor and pulse again. Bake for 15 minutes, remove from the oven and leave in the pan to cool for 5 minutes. Take out the baking beans and then transfer to a wire rack to cool.

sweet chocolate pre-baked pastry shells
To make chocolate pastry shells, follow the basic recipe, and add 2 tablespoons sieved unsweetened cocoa powder to the food processor with the flour. Just before adding the water, add 2 tablespoons sugar to the food processor and pulse again. Bake for 15 minutes, remove from the oven and leave in the pan to cool for 5 minutes. Take out the baking beans and transfer to a wire rack to cool.

stocking your bar

Having a bar area where you can show off your bartending skills and mix cocktails is also a great way of getting your guests to mingle. Try to position it at the furthest point in the room, away from traffic areas—this will help to pull guests into the room, and encourage mixing.

If you stick to three or four cocktail options, you can practice making them ahead of time, so that you have the proportions memorized and the motions mastered. A set cocktail list also allows you to batch major ingredients in advance, for example a pitcher of manhattans. You can then pour the mixture over ice in a glass pitcher, stir and strain into glasses. This is especially useful for those who are not too confident at mixing cocktails in front of their guests, but it only works if there are enough guests to use up the pitcher before the cocktail gets watery.

Make sure you are organized, and have all the tools you will need to hand. You do not want your guests thinking that making them a drink is a lot of work, and they are more likely to ask for a drink if they can see the ingredients set out. Most guests will drink one to two drinks per hour.

Provide mixers such as club soda, tonic, cola, and ginger ale at the bar in pitchers. You should also provide orange juice, grenadine, tomato juice, Tabasco, lemons, limes, and Worcestershire sauce. Try and have a different shaker for each cocktail, so that you do not need to keep washing them between drinks. Borrow from friends for the night if necessary. This will help you assemble drinks quickly, as will setting out the garnishes in glass bowls.

For wine drinkers, have one bottle for every two people, assuming five servings per bottle.

Some people are going to want beer, no matter how appealing the cocktails are, and for them, one six-pack for every two people, assuming 12-fluid ounce servings, should be adequate.

Arrange one or two liquors that can be turned into a variety of cocktails. These could be rum, gin, vodka, scotch, bourbon, or tequila.

Make sure you have enough ice. You will be using it to chill bottles and cans, not just in drinks. Generally, about 1 pound of ice per guest should be adequate.

Have a variety of glasses to hand, depending on the drinks you will be offering. You will need wine glasses for wine, juice and water, straight-sided highballs for tall drinks, tumblers for spirits and juices, and martini glasses. You will probably need twice as many glasses as guests.

An alternative to cocktails might be punch. Similar to sharing a bottle of wine, everyone gets to taste the same drink and can then share the experience. It can also be cheaper.

equipment

There are various tools that you will need for making cocktails. Apart from glasses and a cocktail shaker, the following will be helpful:

- food processor
- juicer
- citrus press
- ice crusher
- strainer
- jigger, measuring device
- zester
- bar spoon
- muddler
- cocktail sticks and drink stirrers
- bottle pourer
- ice cube trays

classic cocktail recipes

manhattan

2 fl. oz. whisky

1 fl. oz. sweet red vermouth

dash of Angostura bitters

ice cubes

maraschino cherry, to decorate

Pour the whiskey, vermouth, and bitters into a mixing glass, add 4 or 5 ice cubes and stir well. Strain into a well-chilled cocktail glass and serve with a maraschino cherry.

mojito

4 mint leaves or 2 sprigs

1 tsp. superfine sugar or sugar syrup

freshly squeezed juice of 1 lime

2 fl. oz. white rum

ice cubes

soda water

lime wedge and star fruit slice, for garnish

Put the mint leaves or sprigs, superfine sugar or sugar syrup, and lime juice in a mixing jug or straight into a tall glass. Muddle until the sugar dissolves and the oils are released from the mint, making it aromatic. Fill a glass with ice cubes, add the rum, and stir well. If using a mixing jug, strain or pour the mix into the glass, and top off with soda water. Serve decorated with a lime wedge, slice of star fruit, and an extra sprig of mint.

gin martini

2 fl. oz. gin

small wedge of lemon

2 drops of extra-dry white vermouth

1 green olive

Thoroughly chill the gin and a martini glass, or place them in the freezer until very cold. Rub the edge of the glass with the lemon wedge. Pour in the gin and add the vermouth. Squeeze the juice from the lemon wedge into the glass. Serve immediately, decorated with a green olive on a cocktail stick while the drink is still really cold.

canapés

Canapés are traditionally served at small gatherings. They are bite-size and can be anything from stuffed mushrooms to pretty little sandwiches.

Thai fish cakes

These spicy and flavorful little fish cakes are wonderful as a starter or as a main course. Serve with soy sauce for dipping.

1 tsp. canola oil, for greasing

1 lb. 2 oz. white fish fillet

1 egg, lightly beaten

2 tbsp. cornstarch

1 tbsp. fish sauce

1–2 tsp. red Thai curry paste, or to taste

1 tsp. seeded and finely chopped red chile

2 tbsp. freshly chopped cilantro

salt and freshly ground black pepper

2 green onions, chopped

soy sauce, to serve

Makes 8–9

Lightly brush an oven tray with canola oil. Chop the fish into ½-inch pieces, and put in a food processor. Pulse until coarsely chopped. Add the egg, cornstarch, fish sauce, curry paste, chile, and cilantro, and season with salt and pepper. Pulse a few times until combined. Mix in the onions. Using your hands, form into small fish cakes about 3 inches in diameter.

Pre-heat the oven to 440°F. Put the fish cakes on the oiled oven tray, set it on the high rack of the oven, and cook for 5 minutes per side, or until lightly browned and cooked through. Keep warm while you cook all the fish cakes. Serve with soy sauce.

You can make your own red Thai curry paste by processing 2 shallots, 2 cloves garlic, 2 red chiles, 1-inch piece fresh ginger, 1 tablespoon fish or soy sauce, 1 teaspoon each ground coriander and cumin, 1 chopped lemongrass stalk, zest and juice of 1 lime, and salt and pepper. Cover and store any surplus in the refrigerator for up to 1 week, or freeze for up to 1 month.

see photo on page 8

NOW TRY THIS

Thai salmon & spinach fish cakes
Replace the white fish with two skinless smoked salmon fillets. Steam 1 cup spinach for a few minutes, until wilted, and stir into the mix after the onions.

Thai tuna fish cakes
Replace the white fish fillet with 2 x 5-ounce cans tuna. Drain and add to the food processor with the other ingredients.

mini bacon & mushroom muffins

These little muffins are delightful with drinks as they
are light and full of flavor.

¼ cup/2 oz. butter, plus extra for greasing

1 cup/4 ½ oz. all-purpose flour

1 tsp. baking powder

1 tsp. salt

1 large egg

1 cup/8 fl. oz. whole milk

1 egg, beaten, for glaze

for the filling

4 tbsp. butter

4 slices smoked bacon, finely chopped

16 small mushrooms, finely chopped, plus
12 extra for topping

1 large onion, finely chopped

salt and freshly ground black pepper

Makes 24

First make the filling. In a small skillet, melt the butter, and sauté the bacon, mushrooms, and onion over a low–medium heat, for 20–25 minutes, or until the juices have evaporated and the bacon is well cooked. Season well. Set aside to cool while you make the muffins.

Pre-heat the oven to 400°F, and grease 2 x 12-cup mini muffin pans with plenty of butter. In a small pan, over a gentle heat, melt the butter and set aside to cool slightly.

In a large bowl, whisk together the flour, baking powder, and salt. In another medium bowl, whisk together the egg, milk, and melted butter. Make a well in the center of the flour mixture and quickly pour in the egg mixture and the filling. Stir gently until just combined, and do not over-mix. Spoon into the muffin cups, ¾ full, and brush the surface with beaten egg. Add half a small mushroom to the top of each one, and bake for 20–22 minutes, until well risen and golden. Let cool in the pan for 5 minutes before turning out onto a wire tray to cool completely. Store in an airtight container until required, and serve warm if possible.

see photo on page 9

NOW TRY THIS

goat cheese & tomato muffins
Omit the filling and the butter from the recipe. Instead, fold ¾ cup/4 ounces cubed goat cheese, ¾ cup/4 ounces chopped sundried tomatoes, and 4 teaspoons fresh thyme into the mix, and bake as before.

cashew nut & cilantro muffins
Omit the filling. Combine 4 teaspoons curry paste, ¾ cup/4 ounces toasted chopped cashew nuts, 4 teaspoons freshly chopped cilantro, and fold into the mixture. Bake as before.

saucy Asian meatballs

These little meatballs are just the right size, bursting with flavor, and ideal for cocktail parties.

a little butter, for greasing
10 oz. ground pork
1 lb. ground beef
1 egg, lightly beaten
½ cup/1 oz. fresh bread crumbs
5 cloves garlic, minced
5 shallots, finely sliced
2 tbsp. ground cumin
1 tbsp. paprika
salt and freshly ground black pepper
2 tbsp. sesame oil, plus extra if needed
1 tbsp. fresh ginger, finely chopped
⅔ cup/5 fl. oz. hoisin sauce
¼ cup/2 fl. oz. rice vinegar
2 tbsp. soy sauce
Makes about 45

Pre-heat the oven to 400°F, and grease a large baking sheet with butter. In a large bowl, mix together the ground pork and beef, egg, bread crumbs, 3 cloves garlic, 3 shallots, cumin, paprika, and plenty of salt and freshly ground black pepper, until well combined. Shape into 1-inch diameter balls. In a large skillet, heat 1 tablespoon sesame oil and over a medium-high heat, fry the meatballs, in batches, for a few minutes each side, until well browned. Add a little more oil if needed. Drain on paper towels. At this stage you can either bake the meatballs immediately, or leave them until cold, cover, and store overnight in the refrigerator.

To cook, spread the meatballs on the baking sheet and bake in the oven for 10 minutes. While the meatballs are baking, make the sauce. In a small pan, heat 2 teaspoons sesame oil, and gently fry 2 shallots, 2 cloves garlic, and the fresh ginger for 5 minutes. Add the hoisin sauce, rice vinegar, and soy sauce, and heat together until just simmering. Continue to simmer for 3 minutes and then remove from the heat. Remove the meatballs from the oven, and transfer to a serving bowl. Pour the sauce over the top, stir once to coat them in the sauce. Provide cocktail sticks for serving, and serve warm or cold.

NOW TRY THIS

saucy tomato & chile meatballs
Serve with a different sauce. Finely chop and fry 1 small onion and 1 clove garlic until softened. Add a 14-ounce can chopped tomatoes, 1 seeded and chopped red chile, and cook for 20 minutes, season well.

saucy, sweet & spicy meatballs
Omit the sauce and instead mix ¼ cup/ 2 ounces tomato ketchup, 2 tablespoons each of maple syrup, and soy sauce, ¼ teaspoon each of ground allspice and dry mustard, and 2 tablespoons water. Bring to a boil and simmer for 5 minutes, stirring constantly.

salt cod fritters with garlic mayonnaise

Salt cod needs to be soaked before cooking, so remember to leave enough time for preparing this recipe. Drain and change the soaking water several times.

generous ¾ cup/6 fl. oz. milk
½ lb. salt cod, soaked for 24 hours
1 potato (about ½ lb.), cooked and mashed
1 shallot, finely chopped
2 tbsp. chopped fresh parsley
freshly ground black pepper
juice of ½ lemon
2 tbsp. all-purpose flour
1 egg, beaten
½ cup/2 oz. dry bread crumbs
sunflower oil, for frying

for the garlic mayonnaise
½ cup/4 oz. mayonnaise
1 ½ cloves garlic, crushed
1 tsp. lemon juice

Serves 4

Bring the milk to a simmer in a medium pan. Add the cod and poach gently for about 10 minutes, until the fish flakes easily. Remove any skin and bones, and flake the flesh into a bowl. Add the mashed potato, shallot, and parsley, and mix well. Season with black pepper and squeeze in lemon juice to taste.

Shape the mixture into 8–12 patties, dust with flour, dip in beaten egg, then coat in bread crumbs. Put on a platter or tray, cover, and chill in the refrigerator for at least 30 minutes.

Meanwhile, combine the mayonnaise, garlic, and lemon juice, and add a grind of black pepper. Transfer to a bowl and set aside. Heat about 1 inch of sunflower oil in a large pan. Add the patties in batches and fry for about 3 minutes on each side, until golden. Drain on paper towels and serve with the garlic mayonnaise.

see photo on page 9

NOW TRY THIS

salt cod fritters with lemon mayonnaise
Prepare the basic recipe, adding ¼ teaspoon grated lemon zest to the mayonnaise in place of the garlic.

salt cod fritters with herb mayonnaise
Prepare the basic recipe, adding 1 tablespoon snipped chives and 2 teaspoons chopped tarragon to the mayonnaise instead of garlic.

salt cod fritters with pesto mayonnaise
Prepare the basic recipe, adding 1 tablespoon pesto to the mayonnaise in place of the garlic and lemon juice.

salt cod fritters with tomato salsa
Prepare the basic recipe, serving the fritters with tomato salsa instead of the mayonnaise.

asparagus summer rolls with hoisin chili dipping sauce

This Vietnamese specialty makes a beautiful and unusual appetizer.

¼ cup/2 fl. oz. hoisin sauce
3 tbsp. chili garlic sauce
1 tbsp. soy sauce
2 tsp. cider vinegar
1 tsp. honey
1 tsp. shredded fresh ginger

summer rolls

24 thin asparagus spears
8 (8-in.) spring roll wrappers
4 red lettuce leaves, shredded
1 cup bean sprouts
1 medium carrot, julienned
6 radishes, sliced
1 red chile, seeded and sliced (optional)
¼ cup/1 oz. chopped fresh mint

Makes 4 servings

Combine all the ingredients for the dipping sauce and let sit at room temperature. Taste and adjust for sweetness. Let stand while preparing the rolls.

Steam the asparagus until tender-crisp, then let cool. Submerge the spring roll wrappers in ¼ cup/2 fluid ounces warm water for about 30 seconds until flexible, then lay out on a board. Prepare the rest of the filling ingredients.

Put one quarter of the filling ingredients in the center of each wrapper roll, placing the asparagus first to ensure that it is on the top of the roll. Fold over the ends, then firmly roll up to seal in the contents, keeping the folds underneath. Cut in half and serve with the dipping sauce.

see photo on page 9

NOW TRY THIS

asparagus summer rolls with nuoc cham dipping sauce

For an alternative dipping sauce, combine juice of 1 lemon and 1 lime, ¼ cup/2 fluid ounces water, 3 tablespoons fish sauce, 2 tablespoons sugar, 3 minced garlic cloves, and 1 thinly sliced bird's eye chile.

jumbo shrimp summer rolls with peanut dipping sauce

Omit the asparagus and use 24 cooked, peeled, and deveined jumbo shrimp, sliced in half horizontally and arranged on top of the finished rolls. For a nutty dressing, add up to 3 tablespoons crunchy peanut butter to the dipping sauce.

Mediterranean stuffed mushrooms

With tomatoes and peppers, garlic and oregano, all the flavors of the warm and sunny Mediterranean are stuffed into these little mushroom bites.

24 medium mushrooms

2 seeded and finely chopped roma tomatoes

½ deli roasted red bell pepper, drained and finely chopped

¼ cup/1 oz. rinsed, pitted, and finely chopped kalamata olives

1 scallion, finely sliced

2 cloves garlic, finely chopped

2 tbsp. freshly chopped parsley

1 tsp. dried oregano

½ tsp. freshly ground black pepper

1 tsp. freshly squeezed lemon juice

2 tsp. olive oil

½ cup/4 oz. feta cheese, finely chopped

Makes 24

Pre-heat the oven to 400°F, and line two large cookie sheets with kitchen foil.

Lightly wipe the mushrooms to clean them, and remove and discard the stalks.

In a medium bowl, stir together the tomatoes, red bell pepper, olives, scallion, garlic, parsley, oregano, black pepper, lemon juice, olive oil, and feta cheese. Spoon the filling into the mushrooms and place them on the cookie sheets. Bake for about 20 minutes, until lightly browned. Serve warm or cold.

NOW TRY THIS

manchego cheese & smoked bacon stuffed mushrooms

Chop 6 strips bacon and finely chop one small onion and 2 cloves garlic. Fry until cooked and the bacon is crispy. Mix with 3 tablespoons each of parsley and bread crumbs and 1 cup/ 4 ounces shredded manchego cheese. Fill mushrooms and bake as before.

goat cheese, beet & walnut stuffed mushrooms

Finely chop, and fry until cooked, 2 shallots, ¼ red bell pepper, 1 scallion and 2 cloves garlic. Cool and mix with 4 ounces goat cheese, 1 finely chopped small cooked beet and 2 tablespoons each of chopped walnuts and bread crumbs. Fill mushrooms and bake as before.

cheese & chorizo croquettes

Croquettes made with spicy chorizo are wonderful served with cocktails.

7 oz. chorizo, finely chopped
½ cup/4 oz. butter
⅔ cup/3 oz. all-purpose flour
1 ½ cups/12 fl. oz. whole milk
1 cup/4 oz. shredded sharp Cheddar cheese
4 tbsp. freshly chopped parsley
salt and white pepper
½ cup/2 ¼ oz. all-purpose flour
2 eggs, lightly beaten
3 cups/6 oz. fresh bread crumbs
vegetable oil for deep-frying

Makes 35

In a large skillet, over a high heat, fry the chorizo for 3–4 minutes, until crispy. Remove from the pan and drain on paper towels.

Melt the butter in the skillet over a medium-high heat, until foaming. Stir in the flour and cook for 2 minutes. Remove from the heat and stir in one-third of the milk. Add the remaining milk, a quarter of a cup at a time, and simmer for 2 minutes while it thickens. Add the cheese, and stir until it has melted. Add the chorizo and parsley. Season well with salt and white pepper, and let cool. Cover and refrigerate for 4 hours, or overnight.

Put the flour on a plate, the beaten eggs in a shallow bowl, and the bread crumbs in another bowl. Flour your hands and shape the chilled mixture into 1 ½-inch long croquettes. Roll each one first in flour, then the egg, allowing the excess to drip off, and then in the bread crumbs. Cover and chill for 30 minutes.

Put enough of the oil in a large, deep pan to come halfway up the sides, and heat until 325°F. Fry the croquettes for about 3 minutes each side, until nicely browned, and drain on paper towels. Serve hot, warm, or cold.

NOW TRY THIS

cheese & bacon
Prepare the basic recipe, omitting the chorizo. Replace with smoked bacon, chopped and cooked until crispy.

cheese & red bell pepper
Omit the chorizo and replace with 1 red bell pepper, finely chopped, and cooked until tender.

cheese & ham
Prepare the basic recipe, omitting the chorizo. Substitute with 5 ounces cooked ham. There is no need to cook the ham before adding it to the sauce with the cheese and parsley.

little crab sandwiches

Small and elegant crab sandwiches are easy to make and excellent for preparing ahead of time.

1 lb. fresh crabmeat, mixture of white and brown (use canned if necessary)

⅔ cup/5 fl. oz. good quality mayonnaise

2 tbsp. sour cream or crème fraîche

zest of 1 lemon

3 tbsp. freshly chopped chives

salt and freshly ground black pepper

24 thin slices bread

watercress, for garnish

Makes 48 triangles

Pick over the crabmeat to ensure there are no pieces of shell. If the crabmeat is canned, squeeze to remove excess water.

Put the crabmeat in a medium bowl, add the mayonnaise, sour cream, lemon zest, chives, and stir until combined. Season to taste with salt and freshly ground black pepper.

Spread the crab mixture over 12 slices of the bread and top with the remaining 12 slices, to make sandwiches. Remove the crusts, and cut each one into tiny triangles, four to each round. Arrange the sandwiches on serving plates, and garnish with the cress.

NOW TRY THIS

tuna & tomato
Omit the crab and chives, and replace with canned tuna, well drained and flaked. Add to the rest of the ingredients with 2 finely chopped skinned, seeded, and well-drained tomatoes.

smoked salmon & lettuce
Mix 10 ounces roasted and flaked salmon fillet with 6 ounces chopped smoked salmon, 5 tablespoons mayonnaise and finely chopped celery, 1 tablespoon chopped chives and capers, and 1 teaspoon lemon zest. Add black pepper, and fill sandwiches, adding lettuce leaves.

tartlets

Little tarts that disappear in two bites
are tasty, sweet, and salty, and ideal
to serve with cocktails.

caramelized onion & apple tarts with Swiss cheese & thyme

Caramelized onions mixed with Swiss cheese is the perfect combination.

24 part-baked 3-in. pastry shells,
(see page 5)

1 tbsp. olive oil

1 small sweet onion, finely chopped

1 ½ tbsp. brown sugar

2 tbsp. red wine vinegar

1 tbsp. butter

1 tsp. vegetable oil

1 red apple, peeled and finely chopped

2 tbsp. freshly chopped parsley

2 eggs, lightly beaten

5 tbsp. crème fraîche

salt and freshly ground black pepper

1 cup/4 oz. finely shredded Swiss cheese

2 tsp. chopped thyme

Makes 24

Line 2 large baking sheets with parchment paper. In a medium pan, heat the olive oil and fry the onion for 20 minutes, until softened. Increase the heat and cook, stirring regularly, for 8–10 minutes until lightly browned. Stir in the sugar and vinegar, and simmer for 5 minutes, until the vinegar has reduced and the mixture has a jam-like consistency. Remove from the heat, and set aside.

In a large skillet, heat the butter and oil, and over a high heat, fry the chopped apple until golden brown. Remove from the heat, add the caramelized onion and parsley, and stir to combine. Let cool.

Heat the oven to 375°F, and place the part-baked pastry shells on the lined baking sheets. Place 1 teaspoon of apple and onion mixture into each one. Whisk the eggs and crème fraîche together, and season well with salt and pepper. Spoon 2 teaspoons of egg mixture into each case, and place 1 generous teaspoon of finely shredded Swiss cheese on top. Bake for 20 minutes until golden brown. Cool slightly, remove from the pan, and serve warm garnished with chopped thyme.

see photo on page 22

see photo on page 22

NOW TRY THIS

sundried tomato & Swiss cheese tarts
Prepare the basic recipe, omitting the apple and onion. Combine 4 ounces drained and chopped sundried tomatoes with the rest of the ingredients, and bake as before.

leek & Swiss cheese tarts
Prepare the basic recipe, omitting the apple, onion, and crème fraîche. Fry 4 chopped leeks for 5 minutes, and cool. Mix with 1 cup/ 8 fluid ounces half-and-half, and the rest of the ingredients, and fill and bake as before.

shrimp & avocado barquettes

Barquettes are small boat-shaped pastry shells that make beautiful appetizers. To make this recipe you will need barquette or 'boat' molds.

1 sheet ready-to-roll pastry

4 ripe avocados, mashed (keep covered until just before serving)

1 cup/8 oz. mayonnaise

¼ cup/2 fl. oz. fresh lemon juice

salt and freshly ground black pepper

2 cups/1 lb. cooked baby shrimp

¼ cup/1 oz. chopped fresh flat-leaf parsley

Makes 24

Preheat the oven to 375°F. To prepare the barquettes, roll out half the quantity of the pastry dough on a lightly floured surface to form a 13-inch square. Using a barquette mold as a guide, trim the pastry, adding ½ inch on either side. Press the pastry into the mold and trim the excess from the sides. Collect the scraps and repeat. Repeat with the remaining half of the pastry dough. Each half should yield 12 barquette shells.

Arrange the barquettes close together on a cookie sheet, and line each with a piece parchment paper and baking beans. Bake blind on the middle shelf of the oven for 15 minutes. Take out of the oven, remove the paper and weights, and return to the oven for 7 minutes, or until the barquettes are golden brown. Transfer to a wire rack to cool. When the molds have cooled enough to be handled, remove the barquettes and cool completely.

Combine the avocados, mayonnaise, and lemon juice until well blended. Season with salt and pepper. Spread the avocado mixture in the base of each barquette, top with a few baby shrimp, and garnish with chopped flat-leaf parsley.

see photo on page 23

NOW TRY THIS

scallop & avocado barquettes
Prepare the basic recipe, replacing the baby shrimp with small seared scallops.

smoked salmon barquettes
Prepare the basic recipe, replacing the avocado mixture with 2 cups/1 pound whipped cream cheese. Top with strips of smoked salmon and garnish with sliced red onions and capers.

smoked haddock barquettes
Prepare the basic recipe, replacing the avocado mixture with 2 cups/1 pound whipped cream cheese. Top with flaked smoked haddock. Garnish with chopped chives.

crab & avocado barquettes
Prepare the basic recipe, replacing the baby shrimp with flaked cooked crabmeat.

wild mushroom, bacon & sweet onion tartlets

Use a variety of wild mushrooms to round out the flavor of these little tarts.

24 part-baked 3-in. pastry shells

2 tbsp. olive oil

1 medium sweet onion, finely chopped

2 tbsp. brown sugar

3 tbsp. red wine vinegar

1 tbsp. butter

2 cloves garlic, minced

8 oz. mixed wild and common mushrooms

2 tbsp. freshly chopped parsley

2 eggs, beaten

5 tbsp. crème fraîche

salt and freshly ground black pepper

Makes 24

Line 2 large baking sheets with parchment paper. In a medium pan, heat 1 tablespoon olive oil and fry the onion for 20 minutes, until softened. Increase the heat and cook, stirring regularly, for 8–10 minutes until lightly browned. Stir in the sugar and vinegar and simmer for 5 minutes, until the vinegar has reduced and the mixture has a jam-like consistency. Remove from the heat, and set aside to cool.

In a large skillet, heat the remaining olive oil and the butter, and over a medium heat, fry the garlic and mushrooms for 5 minutes, stirring regularly. Remove from the heat and stir in the parsley. Let cool, and drain well.

Heat the oven to 375°F, and place the part-baked pastry shells on the lined baking sheets. In a small bowl, whisk the egg and the crème fraîche until smooth, and season well. Place ½ teaspoon of onion mixture in the bottom of each pastry case. Spoon 2–3 teaspoons of egg mixture into each pastry case on top of the onion, and drop a teaspoon of the mushroom mixture gently on top of each one. Bake for 20 minutes, until golden brown and set. Cool slightly, and serve warm.

NOW TRY THIS

feta & olive
Prepare the basic recipe, omitting the mushrooms. Drop a little crumbled feta and a few finely chopped and pitted black olives into the tarts on top of the onion, and bake as before.

Cheddar & mushroom
Prepare the basic recipe, adding a little finely shredded sharp Cheddar cheese at the same time as the mushroom, and bake as before.

stilton & caviar
Prepare the basic recipe, omitting the mushrooms, and adding a little crumbled stilton cheese instead. Bake as before, and garnish with a small amount of caviar just before serving.

red onion & Parmesan tartlets

These simple tartlets are a stunning party piece! If you want to prepare them ahead, make the filling and cut out the pastry rounds in advance, then assemble and bake the tartlets just before you want to serve them.

¼ cup/2 fl. oz. milk

¼ cup/2 fl. oz. light cream

2 cloves garlic, peeled and halved

1 egg yolk

½ tbsp. all-purpose flour

⅓ cup/1 ½ oz. freshly grated Parmesan cheese

9 oz. ready-to-bake sheets puff pastry

2 red onions, each cut into 8 wedges

1 tsp. capers, rinsed

¼ tsp. balsamic vinegar

1 tsp. olive oil

2 tsp. chopped fresh parsley

Makes 8

Pre-heat the oven to 375°F. Grease a baking sheet. In a small saucepan, bring the milk, cream, and garlic to a boil. Remove from the heat and let stand for about 15 minutes. Remove and discard the garlic. Whisk the egg yolk and flour to a smooth paste. Bring the milk and cream back to a simmer, then gradually pour it into the flour mixture, whisking constantly until smooth. Return the mixture to the pan and heat gently for 4–5 minutes, stirring, until creamy. Remove from the heat, stir in the cheese, and season to taste.

Roll out the pastry and cut out 8 x 2 ½-inch rounds. Lay the pastry on a baking sheet and spread the cheese custard over them, leaving a ¼-inch border around the edge. Arrange 2 onion wedges on each tart, then sprinkle capers around them. Whisk together the vinegar and oil and drizzle over the onions. Bake the tarts for 15–18 minutes, until the pastry is crisp and golden. Serve hot, warm, or at room temperature, sprinkled with fresh parsley.

see photo on page 23

NOW TRY THIS

red onion, Parmesan & prosciutto tartlets
Tear 6 wafer-thin slices of prosciutto into pieces. Prepare the basic recipe and nestle pieces of prosciutto among the wedges of onion before baking.

red onion, Parmesan & chive tartlets
Prepare the basic recipe, stirring 1 tablespoon snipped fresh chives into the custard. Sprinkle with more fresh chives, instead of parsley, before serving.

red onion & Parmesan tartlets with olives
Prepare the basic recipe, adding several pitted black olives to each tart.

filo tartlets with cherry tomatoes, basil & ricotta

These crisp, golden tartlets filled with baked ricotta and garlic-flavored tomatoes make an elegant start to any party.

9 oz. (8 sheets) filo pastry
3 tbsp. butter, melted
28 cherry tomatoes
½ cup/4 oz. ricotta cheese
2 tbsp. olive oil
2 cloves garlic, crushed
salt and ground black pepper
handful of fresh basil leaves

Serves 4

Pre-heat the oven to 350°F. Grease a baking sheet.

Cut each sheet of filo pastry in half, lay one cut sheet of filo pastry on a board and brush with melted butter. Lay a second cut sheet on top and brush with more butter. Place 3 or 4 tomatoes in the center of the filo. Add small dollops of ricotta, nestled around and among the tomatoes. Gather the filo around the filling and twist the edges together to make an open tart with a firm collar around the edge. Combine the olive oil and garlic and drizzle this over the tomatoes and ricotta. Season with salt and pepper.

Repeat with the remaining cut pastry sheets and filling. Bake the tartlets on the baking sheet for 15 minutes, until crisp and golden. Serve immediately, sprinkled with fresh basil leaves.

see photo on page 23

NOW TRY THIS

filo tartlets with cherry tomatoes & chives
Prepare the basic recipe, sprinkling the cooked tartlets with 1–2 tablespoons snipped fresh chives in place of the basil.

filo tartlets with cherry tomato & blue cheese or goat cheese
Prepare the basic recipe, using crumbled blue cheese or cubed goat cheese in place of the ricotta.

filo tartlets with cherry tomato & arugula
Prepare the basic recipe, serving the tartlets topped with a handful of fresh arugula leaves in place of the basil.

mini tomato & goat cheese tarts

The growing popularity of goat cheese is well deserved as the tangy flavor combines particularly well with tomatoes and herbs.

2 sheets/17 ½ oz. ready-to-roll puff pastry

2 tbsp. olive oil, plus extra for brushing

2 large onions, finely sliced

4 cloves garlic, finely chopped

salt and freshly ground black pepper

3 tbsp. dry white wine

2 tsp. fresh thyme leaves

½ cup/2 oz. freshly shredded Parmesan cheese

3 Roma tomatoes, thinly sliced

3 tbsp. shredded basil leaves

4 oz. garlic and herb goat cheese

Makes 20–24

Pre-heat the oven to 425°F, and line 2 large baking sheets with parchment paper. Roll one sheet of puff pastry to a 11 x 11-inch square. Using a 1 ½-inch cookie cutter, cut out 10–12 circles. Repeat with the other sheet of puff pastry. Transfer the pastry circles to the lined baking sheets and place in the refrigerator to chill.

In a large skillet, heat the olive oil over a medium-low heat, and fry the onions and garlic for 15–20 minutes, stirring frequently, until the onions are softened. Add ¼ teaspoon each of salt and pepper, the wine, and thyme, and cook for another 10 minutes, until the onions are lightly browned. Remove from the heat.

Using a sharp knife, score a ¼-inch-wide border around each pastry circle. Prick the pastry inside the score lines with a fork, and sprinkle 1 teaspoon of shredded Parmesan and 1 tablespoon of the onion on each tart, staying inside the scored border. Add 1 slice of tomato, brush lightly with olive oil, and sprinkle with basil, salt, and pepper. Crumble a couple of small pieces of goat cheese on top, and bake for 15–20 minutes, until the pastry is golden brown. Serve warm or cold.

NOW TRY THIS

mini tomato & goat cheese tarts with bell peppers
Prepare the basic recipe. Add a little finely chopped cooked green bell pepper to the tart with the goat cheese, and bake as before.

mini tomato & goat cheese tarts with jalapeños and bacon
Prepare the basic recipe. Add a few chopped jalapeños to the tart with the basil, and sprinkle the finished tart with a little crumbled crispy bacon before serving.

wild mushroom, bacon, & sweet onion tartlets
Using a variety of wild mushrooms rounds out the flavor of these little tarts, and the crème fraîche and garlic add to the delicious aroma.

bruschetta & crostini

The difference between these two appetizers is the size of the bread slices. Use small rounds of bread, such as baguettes, for crostini, and larger rustic or sourdough loaves for bruschetta.

cheese garlic bread

Richly flavored garlic bread are a perfect choice to be offered from a platter with drinks at a party.

for the dough

1 ¾ cups/7 ¾ oz. white bread flour

1 tsp. dry yeast

½ tsp. salt

1 tbsp. olive oil, plus extra for oiling

½ cup/4 fl. oz. warm water

for the topping

2 tbsp. olive oil

2 cloves garlic, crushed

5 oz. mozzarella cheese, thinly sliced

freshly ground black pepper

chopped fresh parsley, for garnish

Makes 8

To make the dough, combine the flour, yeast, and salt in a large bowl, and make a well in the middle. Add the oil and water and mix to a soft dough. Put the dough on a lightly floured surface and knead for 5–10 minutes until smooth and elastic. Put in a clean oiled bowl, cover with oiled plastic wrap, and let rise in a warm place for about 1 hour, or until doubled in bulk.

Pre-heat the oven to 425°F and lightly grease a baking sheet. Divide the dough into 8 pieces and roll into rounds or ovals, arranging them slightly apart on the baking sheet.

Then add the topping. Mix the oil and garlic, then drizzle it over the bread. Top with the mozzarella, season with pepper, and bake for about 12 minutes, until golden and bubbling. Serve immediately, sprinkled with fresh parsley.

see photo on page 32

NOW TRY THIS

herb & cheese garlic bread
Prepare the basic recipe, sprinkling the bread with fresh thyme leaves or snipped chives instead of parsley.

cheese garlic bread with pesto
Prepare the basic recipe, spreading about ½ teaspoon pesto on each dough round before drizzling with the garlic oil.

cheese garlic bread with chile
Prepare the basic recipe, sprinkling a good pinch of dried chile flakes over each bread before baking.

mashed pea & ham crostini

Buy a very elegant, narrow baguette to make these crostini. If you can only find larger baguettes, cut the slices in half to make bite-size toasts.

2 shallots, finely chopped

2 tbsp. olive oil, plus extra for drizzling

1 cup/5 ½ oz. frozen peas

2 tbsp. white wine

3 strips prosciutto

salt and freshly ground black pepper

12 thin baguette slices

1 clove garlic, halved

chopped fresh mint, for garnish

Makes 12

Gently cook the shallots in the oil for about 3 minutes, until slightly softened. Add the peas and wine, cover, and cook gently for about 4 minutes, until the peas are tender.

Meanwhile, cut each strip of prosciutto in half widthwise, then slice across to make twelve strips. Put the peas and juices in a food processor, season with salt and pepper, and process to make a chunky purée.

Toast the bread on both sides until golden. Rub one side of each toast with the cut side of the garlic clove, then spoon mashed peas on top and finish with a twist of ham. Drizzle with a little more oil, if desired, and a grinding of black pepper.

Sprinkle the crostini with fresh mint and serve immediately.

see photo on page 33

NOW TRY THIS

mashed pea & Parmesan crostini
Prepare the basic recipe, topping each crostini with shavings of Parmesan cheese in place of the prosciutto.

mashed pea & smoked trout crostini
Gently break a smoked trout fillet into 12 large flakes and top each crostini with a piece in place of the prosciutto.

mashed pea & cherry tomato crostini
Cut 12 cherry tomatoes in half and top each crostini with 2 halves instead of the prosciutto.

mashed pea & chorizo crostini
Use 12 slices of wafer-thin chorizo in place of the prosciutto.

chargrilled zucchini, feta & pea bruschetta

These distinctive bruschetta have a refreshing and delicious combination of zucchini, prosciutto and feta cheese with a hint of garlic.

zest and juice of 2 lemons

4 zucchinis, finely sliced lengthways

4 tbsp. olive oil

salt and freshly ground black pepper

1 rustic loaf or ciabatta, cut into about 24 slices

2 cloves garlic, halved

1 ½ cups/12 oz. feta cheese

1 cup/1 bunch mint leaves, finely chopped

16 slices prosciutto, torn

1 cup/5 ½ oz. fresh or frozen baby peas, blanched and refreshed

Makes 24

In a large bowl, combine the lemon juice, sliced zucchinis, and 2 tablespoons of the oil. Season with salt and freshly ground black pepper and set aside for 15 minutes.

Heat a griddle pan over a medium-high heat. Brush the bread slices with the remaining oil, and grill over a high heat for 1–2 minutes each side until golden and slightly charred. Remove the bread from the griddle, and rub one side of each slice with a cut piece of garlic. Remove the zucchini from the lemon juice, keeping the marinade, and add the slices of zucchini to the griddle pan. Fry for 1–2 minutes each side, or until tender and lightly charred, and set aside to cool. Add the feta, lemon zest and mint to the reserved marinade, season again, and stir until it forms a smooth paste. Spread the feta mixture on to the bread slices, top with the torn prosciutto, cooled zucchini, and peas, and garnish with a little extra lemon zest and mint, if desired. Refrigerate until required.

NOW TRY THIS

salami & herbed goat cheese crostini
Prepare the basic recipe. Top each piece of toast with a slice of herbed goat cheese, a slice of salami, a pitted and chopped kalamata olive, and drizzle with balsamic glaze.

brie, prosciutto, pear & honey pecan bruschetta
Prepare the basic recipe. Top each piece of toast with a thin slice of brie, a slice of prosciutto, a slice of pear, a few toasted honey pecans, and a drizzle of honey.

tomato, basil & balsamic glaze bruschetta
Prepare the basic recipe. Top each piece of toast with sliced cherry tomatoes, a slice of fresh mozzarella, some thinly sliced basil, and a drizzle of balsamic glaze.

crostini with blue cheese & pear

Sharp, salty blue cheese and sweet, juicy pear make a sublime combination on these crunchy little toasts. Creamy Gorgonzola is particularly good, but any blue cheese will work well.

1 pear
12 thin baguette slices
2 ¾ oz. Gorgonzola cheese, thinly sliced
freshly ground black pepper
12 cherry tomatoes, for garnish
Makes 12

Peel and core the pear, then slice it into 12 thin wedges.

Toast the bread until golden on both sides. Top each toast with a sliver of blue cheese, a wedge of pear, and a good grinding of black pepper. Serve immediately with a cherry tomato on top.

see photo on page 33

see photo on page 33

NOW TRY THIS

crostini with blue cheese, pear & pecans
Prepare the basic recipe, topping each crostini with a pecan half.

crostini with blue cheese, pear & arugula or watercress
Prepare the basic recipe, topping each crostini with arugula leaves or a sprig of watercress.

crostini with blue cheese, pear & honey
Prepare the basic recipe, drizzling about ¼ teaspoon honey over each crostini.

crostini with pear & pecorino
Prepare the basic recipe, using shavings of Pecorino in place of the Gorgonzola.

tomato–basil bruschetta

A popular Italian classic, this is both simple to prepare and a joy to eat!

4 or 5 medium, ripe tomatoes, peeled and coarsely chopped

⅓ cup/3 fl. oz. olive oil

3 tbsp. balsamic vinegar

⅛ cup/7 oz. chopped fresh basil or ½ tsp. dried basil

pinch of freshly ground black pepper

1 long baguette or 1 loaf Italian bread, cut into ½-in. slices

4 cloves garlic, sliced in half

freshly grated Parmesan cheese, if desired

Makes 10–12 slices

Drain the tomatoes in a strainer for 20 minutes. Combine the oil, vinegar, basil, and pepper in a large bowl and whisk together. Add the drained tomatoes to the dressing and toss to coat. Allow to marinate for at least 15 minutes, or up to 30 minutes.

Toast the bread slices on both sides on a medium-hot grill. When toasted, rub the cut side of the garlic on the top of each slice. Top each slice with some of the tomato mixture. You may serve this immediately or, if desired, sprinkle with Parmesan cheese and return to the grill, covered, until it melts (it doesn't take long).

see photo on page 33

NOW TRY THIS

angel's bruschetta
Spread the grilled, garlic-rubbed slices with a mixture of 1 minced medium onion, 1 pressed large garlic clove, ½ teaspoon each dried oregano and basil, salt to taste, and 8 ounces thinly sliced mozzarella cheese.

shrimp bruschetta
Spread the grilled, garlic-rubbed slices with a mixture of 1 cup/8 ounces cooked salad shrimp, 2 tablespoons olive oil, 1 tablespoon each of balsamic vinegar and lemon juice, ¼ teaspoon garlic powder, and black pepper.

tuna niçoise crostini

These gorgeous little toasted bread slices are topped with
a mixture of eggs, tuna, tomatoes, and aromatic parsley.

1 baguette, cut into about 24 x ½-in. slices

½ cup/4 fl. oz. olive oil

2 cloves garlic, sliced in half

8 eggs, hard-boiled, roughly chopped

1 ½ cups/12 oz. low-fat cottage cheese

4 tbsp. freshly chopped flat-leaf parsley

2 cups parsley leaves

4 tbsp. freshly squeezed lemon juice

2 tbsp. coarsely chopped capers

2 scallions, thinly sliced

salt and freshly ground black pepper

2 cups/12 oz. halved cherry tomatoes

½ cup/3 oz. quartered pitted mixed olives

8 oz. tuna (in olive oil), drained and flaked

Makes 24

Pre-heat the oven to 400°F. Brush both sides of each baguette slice with a little olive oil and put them on a large baking sheet. Bake for 4–5 minutes each side, until golden brown. Rub each one with a cut piece of garlic, and set aside.

In a large bowl, combine the eggs, cottage cheese, 2 tablespoons of the olive oil, the chopped parsley, 2 tablespoons of the lemon juice, the capers, and scallions. Mash until it becomes a coarse paste, and season.

Toss 4 tablespoons of the olive oil with the remaining parsley leaves, 2 tablespoons lemon juice, the tomatoes, and olives. Season with salt and plenty of pepper, and a little more lemon juice, if desired. Fold in the tuna, keeping it chunky if possible.

Divide the egg salad between the slices, and top with the tuna mixture. Refrigerate until needed.

NOW TRY THIS

prawn & cucumber
Prepare the baguette slices, omitting the garlic. Combine ⅔ cup/5 fluid ounces sour cream, and 2 tablespoons each of tomato ketchup and lemon juice. Top each slice with finely chopped lettuce, cucumber and avocado, and add a little of the cream mixture. Add one large cooked shrimp to each one, and season with black pepper.

lobster & mayonnaise
Prepare the baguette slices, omitting the garlic. Combine ⅔ cup/5 fluid ounces sour cream, and 2 tablespoons each of tomato ketchup and lemon juice. Top each slice with finely chopped lettuce and cucumber, and add a little of the cream mixture. Add a bite-size piece of cooked lobster to each one, season with a few red pepper flakes and black pepper.

smoked salmon crostini

Slices of smoked salmon, nestled on slices of crispy toast, spread with cream cheese, with a hint of dill, is a treat for friends and family alike.

1 crusty baguette, cut into about 24 x ½-in. slices

2 tbsp. olive oil

1 cup/8 oz. cream cheese

2 tbsp. freshly squeezed lemon juice

2 tbsp. fresh dill

1 tbsp. prepared horseradish

salt and freshly ground black pepper

8 oz. smoked salmon slices, cut into small pieces

Makes 24

Pre-heat the oven to 400°F. Brush both sides of each slice of baguette with a little olive oil and place them on a large baking sheet. Bake for 4–5 minutes on each side, until golden brown.

In a medium bowl, mix the cream cheese with the lemon juice, 1 tablespoon of the fresh dill, 1 tablespoon prepared horseradish, and season with salt and freshly ground black pepper. Spread each slice of toast with cream cheese, top with smoked salmon, and sprinkle with a little of the remaining dill. Refrigerate until required.

NOW TRY THIS

goat cheese & fig compote crostini
In a small pan, mix ½ cup/3 ounces dried figs, 4 tablespoons brown sugar, 1 cup/8 fluid ounces dry red wine, ½ teaspoon fresh thyme, and a little salt. Bring to a boil, and simmer for about 10 minutes, until thickened. Cool. Place a lettuce leaf and a thin slice of goat cheese on each toast slice, and top with fig compote. Garnish with thyme.

sundried tomato tapenade
In a food processor, pulse 1 cup/4 ½ ounces pitted kalamata olives, ¾ cup/2 ounces sundried tomatoes, and 2 crushed cloves garlic. Add ⅔ cup/5 fluid ounces extra virgin olive oil, 4 tablespoons drained capers, and ¾ teaspoon dried oregano, and blend until a coarse puree forms. Spread on the toast slices.

little pies

Pies are universally loved. They have enticing fillings with an air of mystery, enclosed in a pastry shell—you never know just how delightful the flavor is going to be.

beef curry puffs

The aromatic zing in these little puff pastry parcels will burst out with the first bite, providing an impressive addition to a cocktail buffet.

1 tbsp. vegetable oil

1 small onion, finely chopped

1 clove garlic, crushed

4 oz. ground beef

2 tbsp. madras curry paste

1 small carrot, finely chopped

¼ cup/1 ⅓ oz. frozen peas

3 tbsp. fresh cilantro, chopped

4 tsp. freshly squeezed lemon juice

a little butter for greasing

3 sheets/1 lb. 10 oz. frozen puff pastry, partly thawed

1 egg, lightly beaten

Makes 24

In a large skillet, heat the oil over a medium-high heat, and add the onion and garlic. Cook for about 5 minutes, stirring occasionally, until softened. Add the ground beef and continue to cook, stirring with a wooden spoon to break up the meat. Add the curry paste, and cook for a further 2 minutes. Add the carrot and ⅓ cup/3 fluid ounces water. Bring to the boil, reduce the heat and simmer for 5 minutes. Add the peas, and simmer for a further 3 minutes, or until the mixture has thickened. Stir in the cilantro and lemon juice. Remove from the heat and set aside to cool.

Pre-heat the oven to 400°F and lightly brush 2 large baking sheets with a little butter. Using a 3-inch cookie cutter, cut out 8 rounds from each pastry sheet. Put 1 rounded teaspoon of beef mixture in the center of each pastry round, and brush around the edge of each one with a little water. Fold the pastry over to enclose the filling, and press the edges together to seal well. Transfer the beef puffs to the baking sheets, and brush with beaten egg. Bake for 20–25 minutes, until lightly browned and puffed. Serve hot or warm.

see photo on page 44

NOW TRY THIS

chicken curry puffs
Substitute chicken for the beef, korma (or mild) curry paste for the madras, and 1 small peeled and diced sweet potato for the carrot and peas.

pork vindaloo puffs
Use ground pork instead of beef. Fry 1 small finely chopped onion until brown and crisp. Grind 1 ½ teaspoons black mustard seeds,

1 teaspoon each of cumin seeds, peppercorns, cardamom seeds, and fenugreek seeds, 1 cinnamon stick, and 2 dried chile pods. Put in a food processor with the onion and 2–3 tablespoons water and pulse to a paste.

sweet potato curry puffs
Substitute 1 small peeled and diced sweet potato for the beef.

Indian samosas

These deep-fried savory pastries make wonderful party food.

2 cups/9 oz. all-purpose flour

1 tsp. salt

¼ cup/2 oz. unsalted butter, melted

⅓ cup/2 ½ oz. plain yogurt

2 large potatoes, peeled and diced

2 carrots, peeled and diced

½ cup/3 oz. frozen peas

2 tbsp. olive oil

1 medium onion, finely chopped

2 cloves garlic, minced

½ tsp. finely grated fresh ginger

½ tsp. mustard seeds

½ tsp. curry powder

1 tsp. salt

2 tsp. fresh lemon juice

2 tbsp. finely chopped fresh cilantro

3 cups/1 ½ pints vegetable oil, for frying

Makes 8

Combine the flour and salt in a large bowl. Stir in the melted butter and yogurt. Gradually add enough water to make a firm dough. Turn onto a lightly floured surface and knead until the dough is smooth and elastic.

To make the filling, put the diced potatoes and carrots in a medium saucepan, bring to a boil and cook for 5–10 minutes, until tender. Add the frozen peas for the last 2 minutes of cooking. Remove from the heat and drain. Heat the olive oil in a large skillet. When the oil is hot, add the onion, garlic, ginger, mustard seeds, curry powder, and salt. Sauté until the onion is soft and translucent. Remove from the heat. Add the potatoes, carrots, and peas. Stir in the lemon juice and cilantro.

On a lightly floured surface, roll out the dough to ¼-inch thick. Using a 4-inch cutter, cut out circles of pastry. The samosa dough should yield 8 rounds. Using a pastry brush, glaze the top edge of the circles with water. Spoon 1–2 tablespoons of filling onto the lower half of each circle. Fold the top over and press the edges to seal. Crimp with a fork. Heat the vegetable oil in a heavy skillet or saucepan. When the oil is hot enough, so that a drop of water bounces on contact, immerse the samosas. Fry until golden and crisp, for about 3 minutes. Drain well and serve hot.

see photo on page 45

NOW TRY THIS

Indian samosas with beef
Prepare the basic recipe, adding 1 pound lean ground beef, browned and drained, to the filling mixture.

Indian samosas with chicken
Prepare the basic recipe, adding 2 cups/ 1 pound cooked, chopped chicken to the filling mixture.

Indian samosas in spring roll wrappers
Prepare the basic recipe, replacing the samosa dough with store-bought spring roll wrappers. Fill each wrapper with 1 tablespoon filling. Using a pastry brush, glaze the edges with water and fold the wrapper in half to encase the filling and form a triangle shape.

Camembert & cranberry filo parcels

Baked Camembert cheese is always a favorite, and with sweet onion and tart cranberry sauce, this combination works a treat.

½ cup/4 oz. butter, plus extra for greasing baking sheets and brushing parcels

4 large sweet onions, finely sliced

4 tbsp. brown sugar

2 tsp. white wine vinegar

2 x 1 lb. 12 oz. packets of filo pastry

2 Camembert cheeses, about 1 lb. 2 oz.

12 tsp. cranberry sauce

Makes 12

Lightly grease 2 large baking sheets with butter.

Melt half the butter in a large skillet, and add the onions, sugar, and vinegar. Cook over a low heat for 25 minutes, stirring occasionally, until the onions are caramelized.

Pre-heat the oven to 400°F. Melt the remaining butter. Unwrap the sheets of filo pastry and cut them into 48 x 6-inch squares. Brushing each square of pastry with melted butter as you work, layer 4 squares, one on top of the other, making a half turn each time to form a star shape. Repeat with the remaining pastry to make 11 more 'stars'.

Cut each Camembert cheese into 6 pieces, and put a piece in the center of each star. Top with the onions, and 1 teaspoon of cranberry sauce. Draw up the pastry to enclose the filling, and pinch well to seal. Place on the baking sheets, and chill in the refrigerator for 30 minutes. Gently brush each parcel with a little melted butter, and bake for 10–15 minutes, until golden brown. Serve hot or warm.

NOW TRY THIS

blue cheese & fig filo parcels
Prepare the basic recipe, omitting the Camembert, and cranberry sauce. Substitute blue cheese and fig compote. Fill and bake as before.

sweet potato & cranberry filo parcels
Prepare the basic recipe, omitting the Camembert. Substitute small cubes of sweet potato, roasted until tender, and cooled. Fill and bake as before.

goat cheese & eggplant filo parcels
Prepare the basic recipe, omitting the Camembert, and cranberry sauce. Substitute goat cheese and small cubes of eggplant, sautéed until tender, and cooled. Fill and bake as before.

southwestern egg rolls

These spicy tortilla wraps are packed with a host of flavors.

3 tbsp. vegetable oil

2 chicken breast fillets, cut horizontally

2 tbsp. red bell pepper, finely chopped

4 scallions, finely chopped

⅔ cup/3 oz. frozen corn

½ cup/5 oz. canned black beans, rinsed and drained

4 tbsp. frozen spinach, thawed and drained

4 tbsp. diced (canned) jalapeño peppers

1 tbsp. chopped fresh parsley

1 tsp. ground cumin powder

1 tsp. hot chili powder

½ tsp. salt

¼ tsp. cayenne pepper

1 ½ cups/6 oz. finely shredded Monterey Jack cheese

10 x 7-in. flour tortillas

vegetable oil, for deep-frying

Makes 20

In a large skillet, over a medium-high heat, heat 2 tablespoons vegetable oil, and fry the chicken for about 5 minutes each side until cooked through. Remove from the pan and drain.

Heat the remaining oil in the skillet, add the peppers and scallions and cook over a medium heat for 2–3 minutes. Dice the cooked chicken and return to the pan with the corn, black beans, spinach, jalapeño peppers, parsley, cumin, chili powder, salt and cayenne pepper. Cook for another 5 minutes, stirring well. Remove the pan from the heat, add the cheese, and stir until melted.

Wrap the tortillas in a moist cloth and microwave on high for 1 ½ minutes, or until hot. Spoon a little mixture into the middle of a tortilla, fold in the ends, and roll the tortilla very tight. Pierce with a wooden cocktail stick to hold together. Repeat with the remaining ingredients until you have 10 egg rolls. Transfer to a plate, cover with plastic wrap, and chill for about 4 hours, or overnight.

Place enough oil in a large pan to come halfway up the sides and heat to 375°F. Deep-fry the egg rolls, in batches, for 12–15 minutes, and drain on paper towels. Slice each one diagonally lengthways, and transfer to a serving dish. Serve warm, with avocado dip, if desired (see variation recipe, page 58).

NOW TRY THIS

southwestern egg rolls with curry spices
Prepare the basic recipe, adding 2 teaspoons garam masala, 1 teaspoon turmeric, and 1 teaspoon ground coriander to the skillet with the rest of the spices.

southwestern egg rolls with sweet potato
Prepare the basic recipe, substituting 1 small peeled and diced sweet potato for the chicken. Fry the cubes for 5 minutes, until tender, and fill and cook the egg rolls as before.

cheese & onion puff pastry pies

Caramelized onions and melted cheese encased in
flaky puff pastry is pure comfort food.

1 tbsp. olive oil
1 large onion, finely chopped
2 large eggs, lightly beaten
1 cup ricotta cheese
½ cup/2 oz. grated mozzarella
½ cup/2 oz. grated yellow Cheddar
salt and freshly ground black pepper
1 packet frozen puff pastry, thawed
1 large egg, lightly beaten

Makes 8

Pre-heat the oven to 375°F. Heat the olive oil in a medium skillet. Sauté the onion until soft and golden, about 10 minutes. Remove from the heat.

In a medium bowl, combine the eggs, cheeses, and onion. Season with salt and pepper to taste. On a lightly floured surface, roll out the puff pastry to ¼-inch thick.

Using a 5-inch cutter, cut out circles of pastry. One packet of puff pastry should yield 8 rounds. Using a pastry brush, glaze the top edge of each circle with water. Spoon 2 tablespoons of the filling onto the lower half of the circle. Fold the top half of the circle over, pressing the edges to seal. Crimp with a fork.

Glaze the pie tops with lightly beaten egg and make 1 or 2 slits. Put the pies on a cookie sheet lined with parchment paper and place in the middle of the oven. Bake for 25 minutes, or until the filling is hot and the crust is golden brown.

see photo on page 45

NOW TRY THIS

cheese, onion & potato puff pastry pies
Prepare the basic recipe, adding 2 large potatoes, peeled, chopped, and boiled until soft, to the filling.

cheese, onion & pesto puff pastry pies
Spread 1 tablespoon fresh basil pesto over the puff pastry rounds, leaving a 1-inch border, before adding the filling.

cheese, onion & sundried tomato puff pastry pies
Add 1 cup/6 ounces drained and chopped sundried tomatoes to the filling.

cheese, onion & mushroom puff pastry pies
Add to the filling 1 cup/8 ounces sliced mushrooms, sautéed in 1 tablespoon unsalted butter, until soft and brown.

Spanish empanadas

You can find empanadas, bursting with local flavors, being served all over Latin America.

2 tbsp. olive oil

2 medium onions, chopped

2 tsp. smoked sweet paprika

½ tsp. hot paprika

½ tsp. crushed red pepper flakes

1 tsp. ground cumin

1 tbsp. white vinegar

1 lb. lean ground beef

1 packet frozen puff pastry, thawed

¼ cup/1 ½ oz. raisins

½ cup/4 oz. pitted green olives, chopped

1 large egg, lightly beaten

Makes 8

Pre-heat the oven to 350°F. Heat the oil in a large skillet, then add the chopped onions and sauté for 3 minutes, until the onions are translucent. Add both paprikas, the red pepper flakes, cumin, and vinegar and stir until well combined. Add the ground beef and cook until the meat is browned. Drain half the fat from the skillet.

On a lightly floured surface, roll out the puff pastry ¼-inch thick. Using a 5-inch cutter, cut out circles of pastry. One packet of puff pastry should yield 8 rounds. Using a pastry brush, glaze the top edge of each circle with water. Spoon 2 tablespoons of filling onto the lower half of the circle. Sprinkle each with the raisins and olives. Fold the top half of the circle over, pressing the edges to seal. Crimp the edge by twisting the pastry inward, from one side to the other. This will prevent the juices from leaking during baking. Glaze the tops of the empanadas with the egg. Prick the crust with a fork near the seam to allow steam to escape. Place the empanadas on a cookie sheet lined with parchment paper, and bake for 25 minutes, or until the filling is hot and the crust is golden.

see photo on page 45

NOW TRY THIS

broccoli empanadas
Prepare the basic recipe, replacing the beef with 2 cups/12 ounces cooked broccoli florets and 1 cup/8 ounces ricotta cheese. Omit the raisins and olives.

chicken empanadas
Prepare the basic recipe, replacing the beef with 1 pound skinless chicken breast, cubed.

sausage empanadas
Prepare the basic recipe, replacing the beef with 1 pound mild Italian sausage, removed from its casing and crumbled.

Spanish empanadas with hard-boiled egg
Prepare the basic recipe, adding 2 hard-boiled eggs, finely chopped, to the filling mixture with the raisins and olives.

Thai spring rolls

Garlic, chile, and ginger are popular Thai flavors, and using a ready prepared red Thai curry paste in these cute little spring rolls makes prep time fast.

1 tsp. sesame oil

½-in. piece fresh ginger, finely chopped

1 clove garlic, finely chopped

1 lb. mixed vegetables including bell peppers, bean sprouts, carrots, Chinese cabbage, and mushrooms, all finely sliced

1 tbsp. soy sauce

1 tbsp. red Thai curry paste

1 scallion, finely sliced

7 oz. cooked chicken, finely chopped

1 tsp. ground cumin

¼ cup Thai basil leaves, shredded

¼ cup cilantro, chopped

8 sheets filo pastry

vegetable oil, for deep-frying

Makes 16

In a large skillet, heat the sesame oil and gently fry the ginger and garlic. Add the vegetables, and stir-fry for about 5 minutes. Add the soy sauce, Thai curry paste, and scallion, and cook for a minute more. Remove from the heat and set aside to cool. Finely chop the chicken, sprinkle with ground cumin, add to the vegetables with the Thai basil leaves and cilantro, and stir to combine.

Trim each sheet of filo pastry until it measures roughly 240 mm x 100 mm, and place a tablespoon of the cooled vegetable mix in the middle at the bottom of the sheet. Brush the edges of the pastry with a little water and start to roll the pastry tightly up over the filling from the bottom. After two or three rolls, fold in the edges to the middle, enclosing the filling. Brush the exposed edges on each side and the far edge with a little more water. Continue to fold the pastry, rolling away from you, and seal well at the end.

Place enough oil in a large wok to come halfway up the sides and heat to 375°F. Deep-fry the spring rolls, in batches, for about 5 minutes, until golden brown. Remove and drain on paper towels. Serve hot or warm.

NOW TRY THIS

duck & hoisin sauce spring rolls
Roast 2 duck breasts for 20 minutes at 350°F, then cool. Remove the skin, slice and shred the duck. Transfer to a bowl, and mix with 2 tablespoons hoisin sauce and 2 sliced scallions. Fill and cook the spring rolls as before.

chicken & vegetable spring rolls
Prepare the basic recipe. Omit the red Thai curry paste, and add 2 tablespoons oyster sauce, 1 tablespoon light soy sauce, and 1 tablespoon Chinese five-spice powder. Fill and cook the spring rolls as before.

shrimp & vegetable spring rolls
Prepare the basic recipe, omitting the chicken, and substituting 7 ounces cooked shrimp. Fill and cook the spring rolls as before.

dips

You can serve almost anything with dips, from plain or fancy chips, to chopped vegetables, or even egg rolls or beef puffs from the previous chapter.

avocado dip with Turkish bread

This dip is especially good with Turkish bread but you could also use pita bread.

2 tsp. fast action yeast

1 tsp. sugar

2 ⅓ cups/10 ½ oz. bread flour

2 tsp. olive oil, plus extra for greasing and brushing

1 tsp. Nigella seeds (black onion seeds)

1 tsp. sesame seeds

8 avocados, very ripe but not bruised, stones and skins removed

2 large beefsteak tomatoes, finely chopped

juice of 3 limes

large bunch cilantro, stalks and leaves chopped

4 scallions, finely sliced

2 green chiles, seeds removed and finely chopped

salt and freshly ground black pepper

Makes 12 servings

For the yeast liquid, put ¾ cup plus 1 tablespoon/7 fluid ounces warm water in a small bowl, add the yeast, sugar and 1 teaspoon of the bread flour, and stir to combine. Set aside for 40 minutes.

For the bread, put the flour in a stand mixer, add the yeast mixture and olive oil, and using the dough hook, knead for 7 minutes. Grease a bowl with olive oil, add the dough, and turn to coat it. Cover and set aside in a warm place for 1–2 hours, until doubled.

Heat the oven to 430°F. Turn the dough out onto a lightly floured worktop, and knead a couple of times. Flatten it and transfer to a floured baking sheet. Gently press out and shape the dough into a rectangle about ¾-inch thick. Using your fingers, create dimples, brush with olive oil, and sprinkle with Nigella and sesame seeds. Bake for 15 minutes, or until golden brown, and cool on wire racks.

Make the dip. Mash the avocado until almost smooth. Stir in the tomatoes, lime juice, cilantro, scallions, and chiles. Season with salt and freshly ground black pepper, transfer to a serving bowl, cover with plastic wrap, and chill until required. Slice the bread and serve with the dip.

see photo on page 56

NOW TRY THIS

avocado ranch dip
Combine the flesh of six peeled and stoned avocados, 1 cup/8 fluid ounces each of mayonnaise and sour cream, 2 tablespoons buttermilk, 3 tablespoons white vinegar, ¼ teaspoon each of salt, dried parsley, onion powder, dried dill weed, garlic powder and black pepper. Serve with the Turkish bread.

California avocado dip
Finely chop 1 small sweet onion, 1 red chile, and ¼ cup/¼ ounce cilantro. Add to the dip with the rest of the ingredients, and serve with the Turkish bread.

bacon & avocado dip
Prepare the basic avocado dip recipe, adding 4 slices chopped grilled bacon.

minty cucumber & yogurt dip

This refreshing dip is based on the classic Greek tzatziki and makes a light, informal appetizer. Serve it with pita bread or chips for scooping.

½ large cucumber
1 cup/8 oz. plain Greek yogurt
1 clove garlic, crushed
2 tbsp. chopped fresh mint
salt

Serves 8

Peel the cucumber, cut it in half lengthways, and scrape out the seeds. Then grate the cucumber and place it in a sieve. Press out as much liquid as possible.

Put the cucumber in a bowl and mix in the yogurt, garlic, and mint. Season to taste with salt. Transfer to a serving bowl and chill until ready to serve.

see photo on page 57

see photo on page 57

NOW TRY THIS

garlicky cucumber & yogurt dip
Prepare the basic recipe, adding an extra clove of crushed garlic.

spicy cucumber & yogurt dip
Prepare the basic recipe, adding 1 seeded and finely chopped green chile.

cucumber, scallion & yogurt dip
Prepare the basic recipe, adding 3 finely sliced scallions.

herb, cucumber & mint dip
Prepare the basic recipe, adding 1 tablespoon snipped fresh chives and 1 tablespoon chopped fresh cilantro with the mint.

roasted red bell pepper & walnut dip

Richly flavored with walnuts and smoky bell peppers, and served with chilled white wine, this is the perfect dip for cocktail parties.

2 large red bell peppers
⅓ cup/1 oz. walnuts
½ tsp. paprika
¼ tsp. ground ginger
good pinch of cayenne pepper
1 clove garlic, crushed
2 tbsp. olive oil
salt
2 tsp. lemon juice
2 tsp. chopped fresh mint

Serves 8

Pre-heat the oven to 450°F. Put the peppers on a baking sheet and roast them for about 30 minutes, until blackened. Put the peppers in a bowl, cover with plastic wrap, and let stand for about 20 minutes, until they are cool enough to handle and the skins have loosened.

Peel and seed the peppers, then put the flesh in a food processor with the walnuts, paprika, ginger, cayenne pepper, garlic, and oil. Season with salt and process to a smooth purée. Stir through the lemon juice, and chopped mint and serve.

see photo on page 57

NOW TRY THIS

creamy roasted bell pepper dip
Prepare the basic recipe, then stir in 3 tablespoons crème fraîche when it has cooled.

roasted red bell pepper & walnut dip with basil
Prepare the basic recipe, adding a small handful of fresh basil leaves to the food processor, and omitting the mint.

roasted red bell pepper with pine nuts & basil
Prepare the basic recipe, using pine nuts in place of the walnuts and adding a small handful of fresh basil leaves. Omit the mint.

roasted red bell pepper & cashew dip
Prepare the basic recipe using cashews in place of the walnuts.

fiery pumpkin dip

This glorious orange dip offers a rich combination of sweet, spicy, fiery, and sour flavors. Be warned, once you start dipping, it's hard to stop.

1 ½ cups/1 lb. 5 oz. pumpkin or butternut squash, seeded, peeled, and cut into chunks

2 tbsp. olive oil

salt and freshly ground black pepper

1 clove garlic, crushed

1 tsp. grated fresh ginger

1 red chile, seeded and finely chopped

juice of ½ lime

Serves 8

Pre-heat the oven to 400°F. Put the pumpkin or squash in a baking dish, drizzle with 1 tablespoon of the oil, and season with salt and pepper. Roast for about 20 minutes, tossing once or twice during cooking, until tender.

Transfer the pumpkin or squash into a food processor and add the garlic, ginger, chile, and remaining oil. Process until smooth, then briefly pulse in the lime juice and check the seasoning.

Scrape the dip into a bowl and serve hot, warm, or cold (it will thicken on cooling, so give it a good stir before serving.)

see photo on page 57

NOW TRY THIS

chunky pumpkin dip
Coarsely mash the pumpkin or squash by hand and stir in the other ingredients to produce a chunkier dip.

spiced pumpkin dip
Prepare the basic recipe, omitting the chile. Add 1 teaspoon ground cumin and 1 teaspoon ground coriander with the garlic and ginger.

curried pumpkin dip
Prepare the basic recipe, adding 1 teaspoon medium curry paste to the cooked pumpkin and the juice of ½–1 lemon instead of lime juice.

spicy pumpkin dip with harissa
Prepare the basic recipe, omitting the chile and adding 1 teaspoon harissa (hot chile paste) and 1 teaspoon ground cumin instead.

smoky chipotle hummus with garlic bagel chips

Hummus is amazingly versatile. You can flavor it with garlic, chile, and different spices.

6 savory bagels, any flavor

⅓ cup/3 fl. oz. plus 2 tbsp. extra virgin olive oil

½ tsp. granulated garlic, or garlic powder

1 tsp. sea salt

2 x 14-oz. cans chickpeas, drained

¼ cup plus 2 tbsp./6 oz. tahini

4 tbsp. freshly squeezed lemon juice

1 tbsp. canned chipotle chiles, minced

2 cloves garlic, minced

1 ½ tsp. ground cumin

4-oz. jar sliced pimientos in oil, drained

½ cup/⅓ oz. freshly chopped cilantro

salt and freshly ground black pepper

Makes 20 servings

First make the bagel chips. Pre-heat the oven to 250°F. Slice the bagels thinly, no thicker than ⅛–¼ inch. Transfer the slices to a large mixing bowl. In a small bowl, whisk ⅓ cup/3 fluid ounces of the olive oil and the garlic together, and drizzle over the bagel slices. Using your hands, toss the slices around in the oil, until they are evenly coated. Sprinkle with salt, and toss again. Arrange the bagel slices on two large baking sheets, in one layer, and bake for 35 minutes, until the slices are crisp. Store in an airtight container for up to 1 week.

Make the hummus. In a food processor, blend the chickpeas with ½ cup/4 fluid ounces water, the tahini, lemon juice, 2 tablespoons olive oil, the chiles, garlic, cumin, pimientos, and cilantro. Season to taste with salt and freshly ground black pepper. Transfer to a serving bowl or an airtight container, and store overnight, or up to 2 days, in the refrigerator. Serve with the bagel chips.

NOW TRY THIS

za'atar flavored hummus
Prepare the basic recipe, omitting the chipotle chiles and ground cumin. Substitute 1 teaspoon of the spice za'atar, and serve as before.

roasted garlic & red chile hummus
Prepare the basic recipe, omitting the chipotle chiles and ground cumin. Add the flesh squeezed out from one roasted garlic bulb, and 1 roasted red chile to the food processor with the rest of the ingredients. Serve as before.

sundried tomato hummus
Prepare the basic recipe, adding ¼ cup/ 2 ounces sundried tomatoes, drained, to the food processor with the rest of the ingredients. Serve as before.

grilled
or fried

An exciting array of amazing flavors and textures are found in this chapter, from deep-fried risotto balls, to chicken tenders. Served either warm or cold, they are equally delicious.

mini vegetable frittata

These frittata are bite-size omelettes, with pasta, scallions, bell peppers, peas and Cheddar cheese, full of fun and flavor.

butter for greasing

6 oz. small pasta shapes, such as orzo

3 tbsp. olive oil

9 scallions, finely sliced

2 cloves garlic, minced

1 ½ red bell peppers, seeded and finely chopped

½ cup/2 ½ oz. frozen peas

10 eggs

½ cup plus 2 tbsp./5 fl. oz. whole milk

2 tsp. dried oregano

salt and freshly ground black pepper

1 ½ cups/6 oz. Cheddar cheese, finely shredded

Makes 24

Generously grease 2 x 12-cup non-stick muffin pans with butter.

Cook the pasta shapes in lightly salted water, according to the packet instructions, for about 8 minutes. Rinse with cold water, drain well, and transfer to a large bowl.

Pre-heat the oven to 400°F. Put the olive oil in a large skillet, and add the scallions, garlic, red bell peppers, and peas. Fry over a medium heat for 5 minutes, remove from the heat, and cool. Add to the pasta.

In a large bowl, whisk the eggs, milk, oregano, and plenty of salt and freshly ground black pepper. Divide the pasta mixture between the muffin pans, sprinkle in the cheese, and pour over the egg mixture. Bake for 20–25 minutes, until golden brown. Use a small knife to loosen the fritatta around the edges, as they may stick slightly. Serve warm or cold.

see photo on page 64

NOW TRY THIS

mini vegetable frittata with corn
Prepare the basic recipe, omitting ⅓ of the red bell pepper and all the peas. Substitute ½ cup/5 ounces frozen corn.

mini vegetable frittata with ham
Prepare the basic recipe, omitting ⅓ of the red bell pepper and half the peas. Substitute 3 ounces chopped ham.

mini vegetable frittata with feta cheese
Prepare the basic recipe. Crumble in 6 ounces feta cheese in place of the Cheddar.

mini vegetable frittata with bacon
Prepare the basic recipe, omitting ⅓ of the red bell pepper and half the peas. Substitute 3 slices grilled bacon.

deep-fried risotto balls with melting mozzarella

These rich, creamy risotto balls are an indulgent feast of an appetizer. Serve them with a fresh, tangy tomato or fruit salsa.

2 tbsp. olive oil
1 small onion, finely chopped
1 clove garlic, crushed
⅔ cup/4 oz. risotto rice
⅓ cup/3 fl. oz. white wine
1 ⅔ cups/13 fl. oz. cups boiling vegetable or chicken stock
⅓ cup/1½ oz. grated Parmesan cheese
2 tbsp. chopped fresh flat-leaf parsley
salt and freshly ground black pepper
3 oz. mozzarella, cut into 12 small cubes
12 large basil leaves
sunflower oil, for deep-frying

Makes 12 balls

Heat the olive oil in a large pan, then gently fry the onion and garlic for about 4 minutes, until soft but not brown. Add the rice, stir for 2 minutes, pour in the wine and simmer, stirring, until absorbed. Add the stock and stir frequently for about 20 minutes, until the stock is absorbed and the risotto is creamy. Stir in the Parmesan, parsley and seasoning. Let cool.

Divide the cooled rice into 12 portions. Wrap each cube of mozzarella in a basil leaf. Press a portion of rice around each cube. Place on a board and let stand for at least 30 minutes. Pour oil into a deep pan until it is two-thirds full. Heat the sunflower oil to 375°F, or until a cube of bread turns brown in about 1 minute. Deep-fry the risotto balls in batches, for about 3 minutes, until crisp and golden. Drain on paper towels and serve hot.

see photo on page 65

NOW TRY THIS

deep-fried risotto balls with sage & mozzarella
Prepare the basic recipe, adding 2 teaspoons chopped fresh sage in place of the parsley. Omit the basil leaves from the filling.

deep-fried risotto balls with melting blue cheese
Prepare the basic recipe, using cubes of blue cheese in place of the mozzarella. Omit the basil leaves from the filling.

deep-fried herbed risotto balls with melting mozzarella
Prepare the basic recipe, stirring 2 tablespoons snipped fresh chives and 2 teaspoons chopped fresh mint into the risotto with the parsley.

beef skewers with béarnaise sauce

Use really good quality steak for this recipe, and you will be rewarded with tender and tasty beef served with the best sauce of all, béarnaise.

1 ¼ cups/10 oz. butter

2 tbsp. white wine vinegar

2 small shallots, finely chopped

8 sprigs fresh tarragon, 4 sprigs whole and 4 chopped

4 egg yolks

¼ cup/2 fl. oz. plus 1 tsp. freshly squeezed lemon juice

salt and freshly ground black pepper

½ cup/⅓ oz. freshly chopped cilantro

2 cloves garlic, crushed

2 tbsp. olive oil, plus extra for serving

2 tsp. ground coriander

2 tsp. ground cumin

¼ tsp. ground cinnamon

2 lb. beef tenderloin or sirloin, cut into 1-in. pieces.

Makes 12 skewers

Make the béarnaise sauce by melting the butter slowly in a pan over a low heat. Skim off any foam, cooking until no more foam appears. Strain through a sieve lined with paper towels, and cool.

In a small pan, heat the vinegar with the shallots, 4 tarragon sprigs and 2 tablespoons of water. Bring to a boil and simmer gently until the liquid has almost evaporated. Whisk in the egg yolks, and keep whisking over a low heat until the yolks emulsify and thicken, about 3–5 minutes. Remove from the heat and add the cooled butter in a thin stream, whisking continuously until you have a thick sauce. Pass through a fine sieve and discard the solids. Add 1 teaspoon of lemon juice, the remaining chopped tarragon, seasoning, and set aside.

Put the cilantro, lemon juice, garlic, olive oil, ground coriander, cumin, and cinnamon in a small bowl. Add the beef and toss to coat. Cover and refrigerate for 1 hour. Thread the beef onto small soaked bamboo skewers. Sprinkle with salt and black pepper.

Pre-heat a griddle on a medium-high heat. Brush the skewers with the marinade, and cook for 2–3 minutes each side for medium. To serve, drizzle with a little olive oil, and cover loosely with aluminum foil to rest for 5 minutes. Serve warm with the sauce for dipping.

NOW TRY THIS

jerk chicken skewers with honey mustard sauce

Thread 2 pounds cubed chicken breasts onto the skewers, and marinate. Make sauce by mixing ¾ cup/3 fluid ounces sour cream, ⅓ cup/2 ½ ounces mayonnaise, ⅓ cup/2 ½ ounces Dijon mustard, ⅓ cup/3 fluid ounces honey, and 4 teaspoons lemon juice together. Cook the chicken as before, and serve with the sauce.

beef skewers with horseradish sauce

Substitute the marinade with 3 tablespoons fresh rosemary leaves and 4 tablespoons olive oil. Substitute the béarnaise sauce with ½ cup/4 ½ ounces natural yogurt, 4 tablespoons finely shredded horseradish, and season to taste.

Thai chicken satay skewers

Creamy peanut sauce with tender skewered chicken is a deservedly popular Thai classic.

1 lb. boneless, skinless chicken breasts

for the marinade

⅓ cup/3 fl. oz. soy sauce

2 tbsp. fresh lime juice

2 cloves garlic, pressed

2 tsp. grated fresh ginger

1 tsp. crushed red pepper flakes

for the peanut sauce

¾ cup/6 fl. oz. canned unsweetened coconut milk

1 tbsp. creamy peanut butter

4 green onions with tops cut into 1-in. pieces

Makes 36 skewers

Cut the chicken into ¼-inch-wide strips and put in a shallow dish. Make the marinade. Combine the soy sauce, lime juice, garlic, ginger, and red pepper flakes in a bowl. Set aside 3 tablespoons of the mixture; cover and refrigerate. Mix in 2 tablespoons water to the remaining mixture. Pour over the chicken and toss to coat. Cover the chicken and marinate in the refrigerator for between 30 minutes and 2 hours, stirring occasionally.

Preheat a grill to medium. Meanwhile, combine the coconut milk, the reserved marinade, and peanut butter in small saucepan. Bring to a boil over a medium-high heat, stirring constantly. Reduce the heat and simmer for 2–4 minutes, until the sauce thickens. Keep warm. Drain the chicken and discard the marinade. Weave 3–4 chicken strips accordion-style onto each of 36 soaked bamboo skewers, alternating with green onion pieces. Grill the skewers on the uncovered grill for 6–8 minutes or until the chicken is cooked. Turn halfway through grilling time. Serve with warm peanut sauce for dipping.

see photo on page 65

NOW TRY THIS

Malaysian pork satay
Replace the chicken with 1 pound pork tenderloin. For the marinade, replace the soy sauce, lime juice, red pepper, and water with 1 cup finely minced shallots, 1 teaspoon each of ground coriander, salt, and cumin, and 1 tablespoon each of ground turmeric, sugar, and cooking oil.

Thai prawn satay
Replace the chicken with 1 pound prawns. For the marinade, replace the soy sauce, lime juice, ginger, pepper flakes, and water with 1 tablespoon each of palm sugar, soy sauce, white pepper, Golden Mountain sauce (or Maggi seasoning sauce), and oyster sauce, and 1 teaspoon Thai curry powder.

bacon & Cheddar sliders

These baby hamburgers have that wonderful combination of bacon and Cheddar cheese, and are an ideal size for parties.

12 oz. ground sirloin

3 shallots, finely chopped

1 tsp. Dijon mustard

salt and freshly ground black pepper

cooking spray

½ cup/2 oz. grated Cheddar cheese

8 whole wheat slider buns

3 tbsp. mayonnaise

4 small dill pickles, cut lengthwise into 4

4 small lettuce leaves, cut into 2

1 ripe tomato, cut into 8 slices

3 slices bacon, cooked until crispy, and cut into 1-in. pieces

Serves 8

Gently mix the sirloin with the shallots, Dijon mustard, salt and plenty of freshly ground black pepper. Divide into 8 portions and form into patties.

Spray the grill with cooking spray, and place the patties on the grill. Cook for 2–3 minutes each side, topping each one with 1 tablespoon grated cheese during the last minute of cooking.

Spray the cut sides of the slider buns and grill until nicely toasted. Spread the bottom half of each bun with mayonnaise, add a patty, two slices of dill pickle, ½ lettuce leaf, 1 slice of tomato, and bacon pieces. Season with freshly ground black pepper, and top with the other half of the slider buns. Serve immediately.

see photo on page 65

NOW TRY THIS

California sliders with guacamole
Omit the mayonnaise, dill pickles, lettuce, and bacon. Mash 2 avocados with the juice of ½ lime. Stir in 1 tablespoon freshly chopped cilantro, 1 minced clove garlic, ½ teaspoon salt, and ¼ teaspoon cayenne pepper. Spread the slider buns with butter and grill as before. Assemble the sliders with the guacamole and cheese on top of the patties.

dixie burgers with chow chow dressing
Omit the dill pickles and bacon, and substitute chow chow dressing, made by mixing ½ cup/ 4 fluid ounces chow chow with 3 tablespoons mayonnaise.

buffalo chicken sliders
Omit the dill pickles and bacon. Assemble the sliders using Buffalo Chicken tenders (see page 74), and the rest of the ingredients.

potato rosti with smoked salmon

These little rounds of crispy fried potato are absolutely delicious served with just a sprinkling of sea salt, but you can jazz them up by topping them with sour cream and smoked salmon.

2 lb. potatoes, peeled and coarsely shredded

3 tbsp. butter

2 eggs, lightly beaten

2 tbsp. flour

salt and freshly ground black pepper

1 tbsp. goose fat or olive oil

1 ¼ cups/10 fl. oz. sour cream

8 oz. smoked salmon slices, cut into small pieces

fresh dill, for garnish

Makes 36

Place the peeled and shredded potato in a clean dish towel and squeeze out as much of the moisture as you can. Transfer to a large bowl. Melt 2 tablespoons of the butter in a small pan, cool, and add to the potato with the eggs, flour, and plenty of salt and freshly ground black pepper.

Heat the remaining butter and goose fat in a large skillet over a medium-high heat, add tablespoonfuls of the potato mix, and assemble them into small rounds, flattening them slightly with a spatula. Fry for 3–4 minutes each side, or until crisp and golden, and transfer to paper towels to drain. Sprinkle with a little salt. Repeat with the remaining potato mixture. When cooled, top with a small dollop of sour cream and a small piece of smoked salmon. Sprinkle a little fresh dill over the top and serve immediately.

NOW TRY THIS

sweet potato rosti with mascarpone & prosciutto
Prepare the basic recipe, substituting sweet potatoes for the potatoes, mascarpone for sour cream, and prosciutto for the smoked salmon.

potato rosti with onion & goat cheese
Prepare the basic recipe, adding 1 small finely chopped onion to the mixture with the egg.

When cooked, top with a slice of goat cheese, and sprinkle with freshly chopped parsley.

cheese & onion potato rosti with ham
Prepare the basic recipe, adding ½ cup/ 2 ounces finely shredded sharp Cheddar cheese and 2 finely chopped scallions with the egg. Cook as before. Just before serving, top with a shaved ham and sprinkle with parsley.

buffalo chicken tenders

A classic choice for game nights, these are also excellent for cocktail parties, as they are real crowd pleasers, especially with a blue cheese dip.

for the dip
1 ½ cups/6 oz. crumbled blue cheese
½ cup/4 fl. oz. buttermilk
salt and freshaly ground black pepper

for the chicken
1 ½ cups/6 ¾ oz. all-purpose flour
2 tsp. garlic powder
2 tsp. cayenne pepper
¾ cup/6 fl. oz. buttermilk
salt and freshly ground black pepper
¾ cup/6 fl. oz. vegetable oil
2 lb. chicken tenders
⅔ cup/5 fl. oz. hot sauce
3 tbsp. butter, melted
Makes 12 servings

First make the dip. In a medium bowl, mix the crumbled blue cheese with the buttermilk, and season to taste with salt and freshly ground black pepper. Set aside.

Pre-heat the oven to 250°F. In a medium bowl, mix the flour with the garlic powder, and cayenne pepper. Put the buttermilk in a separate bowl, and season both bowls with salt and freshly ground black pepper. In a large skillet, heat the oil over a medium-high heat. Working quickly, dip the chicken tenders first in the buttermilk, allowing the excess to drip off. Next, roll them in the flour, then back in the buttermilk and then once more in the flour. Transfer the chicken immediately to the hot oil, and fry for 3–4 minutes each side, in batches, until golden brown and cooked through. Do not crowd the pan, and keep warm in the oven while you cook the remaining chicken.

In a medium bowl, mix the hot sauce with the melted butter, add the chicken, and toss to coat. Serve warm.

NOW TRY THIS

breaded buffalo chicken tenders baked in the oven
Dip the chicken tenders first in flour, then beaten egg, and panko bread crumbs. Put on a parchment-lined baking sheet, and bake at 400°F for 8 minutes each side, or until cooked through. Serve with the dip as before, warm or cold.

buffalo breaded goat cheese baked in the oven
Slice 1 pound goat cheese and form into balls. Roll first in flour, then beaten egg and bread crumbs. Fry for 3 minutes each side, or until golden brown. Make a dip with 1 cup/ 8 ounces orange marmalade, 4 teaspoons white wine vinegar, and 1 teaspoon crushed red pepper flakes.

grilled scallops wrapped in prosciutto

The prosciutto really enhances the flavor of the scallops in this recipe. Helen, my expert on fish, says that some people like the coral, or roe, on a scallop, but personally I prefer it trimmed away.

10 slices paper-thin prosciutto, about 8 oz.

20 medium scallops, about 1 lb.

salt and freshly ground black pepper

¼ cup/2 fl. oz. extra virgin olive oil, for drizzling and cooking

2 lemons, cut into wedges, for serving

Makes 20

Cut each slice of prosciutto in half lengthwise. If leaving the corals on the scallops, prick them or they will burst during cooking. Wrap each half slice of prosciutto around the sides of one scallop, overlapping the prosciutto ends. Repeat with all the scallops.

Season with salt and freshly ground black pepper, and drizzle with a little olive oil. Heat the remaining oil in a large skillet over a medium-high heat, and cook the scallops in batches, for 1 ½ minutes on each side, until just opaque. Slide each scallop onto a small wooden skewer, with a lemon wedge, and serve immediately.

NOW TRY THIS

scallops with green Thai curry paste wrapped in zucchini
Omit the prosciutto. Cut long strips of zucchini using a vegetable peeler or cheese slicer. Smear the scallops with a little green Thai curry paste and wrap them in zucchini, securing with a cocktail stick. Cook as before.

scallops wrapped in nori, with a touch of wasabi & fried in ginger
Omit the prosciutto and substitute with nori. Smear the scallops with a little wasabi paste and add ½-inch piece of fresh ginger, finely chopped, to the oil in the pan while cooking the scallops.

sweet treats & petit fours

Even cocktail parties should have dessert, and here you will find sweet delights to please everyone. From caramel popcorn to little mint chocolates, send all your guests home with lovely memories of a truly delightful evening.

caramel coconut popcorn

This recipe has lots of toasted coconut sprinkled over the top of a mixture of popcorn and marshmallows. Gooey and delicious!

2 ½ cups/7 ½ oz. sweetened shredded coconut, toasted

14 cups/3 lb. popped popcorn

⅔ cup/5 oz. butter

1 ½ cups/12 oz. brown sugar

4 tbsp. light corn syrup

1 tsp. vanilla extract

4 cups/10 oz. marshmallows

Makes about 16 cups

Pre-heat the oven to 350°F. Spread the sweetened shredded coconut out in a single layer on a metal baking pan. Bake for 3–5 minutes, watching closely so that the coconut doesn't burn. Remove from the oven when the coconut is just a light golden brown, and set aside to cool.

Line 2 large cookie sheets with waxed paper. Put the popcorn in a large bowl. In a large pan, over a gentle heat, stir together the butter, brown sugar, corn syrup, and vanilla. When the butter has melted and the sugar has dissolved, increase the heat to medium-high and bring to a boil. Boil for 1 minute, add the marshmallows, and stir until smooth. Remove from the heat, pour over the popcorn, and stir gently to combine. Spread out on the paper-lined cookie sheets and sprinkle with the toasted coconut. Let cool before serving. This can be stored for just 1 or 2 days.

see photo on page 78

NOW TRY THIS

caramel coconut popcorn with bacon
Prepare the basic recipe. Once the popcorn has cooled, add 8 strips bacon, cooked until crispy and crumbled. Stir to combine.

chocolate caramel coconut popcorn
Prepare the basic recipe. In a heatproof bowl, set over a pan of barely simmering water, melt 3 cups/1 pound 2 ounces semisweet chocolate chips, and stir until smooth. Pour over the popcorn, and stir gently to combine. Let cool.

caramel coconut popcorn with cherries
Prepare the basic recipe. In a heatproof bowl, set over a pan of barely simmering water, melt 3 cups/1 pound 2 ounces white chocolate chips, and stir until smooth. Pour over the popcorn with ⅔ cup/4 ounces dried cherries, and stir gently to combine. Let cool.

mini s'mores doughnuts

These mini doughnuts are a perfect way to end an evening!

cooking spray

½ cup/2 ¼ oz. all-purpose flour

¼ cup/2 oz. superfine sugar

2 tbsp. unsweetened cocoa powder, sifted

¼ tsp. baking powder

¼ tsp. baking soda

½ tsp. salt

3 tbsp. plain Greek yogurt

1 ½ tbsp. whole milk

1 large egg, room temperature

2 tbsp. canola oil

2 tsp. vanilla extract

3 tbsp. unsalted butter

2 cups/4 ½ oz. white mini marshmallows

2 cups/8 oz. confectioners' sugar, sifted

3 tbsp. graham cracker crumbs

¼ cup/1 ½ oz. semisweet chocolate chips, melted

Makes 12

Spray a 12-cup mini-doughnut pan with oil. Pre-heat the oven to 350°F.

In a large bowl, whisk together the flour, sugar, cocoa powder, baking powder, baking soda, and ¼ teaspoon salt. In a separate bowl, whisk together the yogurt, milk, egg, canola oil, and 1 teaspoon vanilla extract. Pour into the flour mixture and stir. Using a pastry bag (or use a plastic bag with the corner cut off), fill the doughnut cups two-thirds full. Bake in the oven for about 10 minutes, or until a toothpick inserted in the center comes out clean. Let cool in the pan for 5 minutes, then transfer to a wire rack to cool.

Make the frosting. In a small pan, over a medium heat, melt the butter, ¼ cup/2 fluid ounces water and 1 teaspoon vanilla extract, stirring occasionally. Add the marshmallows and stir until they have melted and the mixture is smooth. In a medium bowl, whisk the confectioners' sugar and remaining salt, and pour the melted marshmallows over, whisking until combined. Dip half of each doughnut into the frosting and put on the rack to drain. Sprinkle each one with graham cracker crumbs and drizzle with melted semisweet chocolate.

NOW TRY THIS

mini doughnuts with chocolate frosting
Prepare the base recipe, omitting the glaze and topping. In a small pan, melt ½ cup/4 ounces butter, 2 tablespoons milk, 1 tablespoon half and half, 1 teaspoon light corn syrup, and 1 teaspoon vanilla extract. Add ⅓ cup/ 2 ounces semisweet chocolate chips and stir until smooth. Dip the top of the doughnuts into the frosting and place on a wire rack to set.

mini doughnuts with sweet berry icing
Prepare the basic recipe, omitting the glaze and topping. Push 2 ounces fresh raspberries through a sieve into a bowl, leaving just the seeds behind. Slowly add 1 ½ cups/6 ounces sieved powdered sugar, stirring until smooth. Dip the top of each doughnut into the glaze, and leave until set. Drizzle with melted semisweet chocolate.

salted caramel and coffee profiteroles

These profiteroles are absolutely divine.

¼ cup/2 oz. butter

1 cup/2 ¼ oz. all-purpose flour

2 eggs, lightly beaten

1 ¼ cups/10 fl. oz. heavy cream

2 cups/8 oz. powdered sugar, divided

3 tbsp. Kahlua or other coffee liqueur

½ cup/8 oz. canned dulche de leche, divided

2 tbsp. whole milk

1 tsp. instant coffee powder mixed with 2 tsp. boiling water

½ tsp. glycerine

Makes 20

Pre-heat the oven to 450°F. In a medium pan, gently melt the butter with ⅔ cup/5 fluid ounces water, until the butter has melted. Bring to a boil, remove from the heat and quickly add the flour. Stir briskly with a wooden spoon until it has all been incorporated, and the mixture comes together in a ball. Return to the heat and beat for 1 minute. Let cool slightly, and add the eggs, a little at a time, beating well after each addition, until you have a smooth, pipeable dough. Transfer the mixture to a piping bag fitted with a ½-inch plain nozzle, and pipe 20 small mounds onto the lined baking sheets, about 1-inch apart.

Bake for 10 minutes, and turn the oven down to 375°F. Bake for another 10 minutes, or until risen and golden. Remove from the oven and make a little hole in the side of each bun. Cool completely on a wire rack.

In a medium bowl, whisk the cream with ½ cup/2 ounces powdered sugar, and the Kahlua, until it forms soft peaks. Cut the profiteroles in half and place a teaspoon of caramel in the base of each. Transfer the cream to a piping bag with a ½-inch nozzle, and pipe a swirl of Kahlua cream on top. For the glaze, sift 1 ½ cups/6 ounces powdered sugar into a medium bowl, add 2 tablespoons milk, the remaining caramel, the instant coffee mix, and glycerine. Beat until smooth. If it is too runny, add a little more powdered sugar; if it is too thick, add more milk. Spread a little glaze on the tops of the profiteroles and place them back on the bases. Chill in the refrigerator until ready to serve.

NOW TRY THIS

choca mocha profiteroles

Prepare the basic recipe, omitting the Kahlua. Melt 8 ounces semisweet chocolate, and cool until it is still liquid but not too hot. Whip the cream until soft peaks form. Stir half the whipped cream into the chocolate and blend with a spatula. Scoop the remaining cream into the chocolate and fold in until blended. Omit the caramel and pipe on the chocolate cream. Top with glaze as before.

banoffi profiteroles

Prepare the basic recipe, adding 1 thin slice banana to the profiteroles on top of the caramel before the cream is piped on. Omit the Kahlua from the filling and the coffee from the glaze.

chocolate french fancies

These little tarts have a delicious sweet chocolate pastry.

2 ¾ cups/12 oz. all-purpose flour

¼ cup/1 oz. unsweetened cocoa powder, sifted

¾ cup/6 oz. butter, plus a little extra for greasing (½ cup/4 oz. cold from the fridge and cubed)

¼ cup/2 oz. shortening, cold from the fridge and cubed

¼ tsp. salt

3 tbsp. superfine sugar

6 oz. semisweet chocolate

2 oz. milk chocolate

⅔ cup/5 fl oz. whipping cream

1 tsp. vanilla extract

1 egg yolk

½ cup/4 fl. oz. caramel

1 cup/8 fl. oz. heavy cream

2 tbsp. confectioners' sugar

Makes 45

Lightly grease 4 x 12 mini muffin pans with a little butter. In a food processor, pulse the flour, cocoa, ½ cup/4 ounces of the butter (cold from the fridge and cubed), shortening, and salt, until it resembles coarse bread crumbs. Add the sugar and pulse again briefly.

Add 5 tablespoons iced water, pulse, add another tablespoon and pulse again until a dough comes together, adding extra water if necessary. Turn the dough out onto a lightly floured worktop, and knead into a round. Roll out to just under ⅛-inch thick, and cut out rounds with a 2 ¼-inch plain cutter. Line the pan cups with the pastry, then chill in the refrigerator for 30 minutes.

Pre-heat the oven to 400°F. Place a few baking beans in each pastry case, and bake for 15 minutes. Remove from the oven, take out the baking beans and transfer the pastry shells to a wire rack to cool.

Make the filling. Gently heat the chocolate, whipping cream, and vanilla until the chocolate has melted. Cool slightly, and beat in the remaining butter a little at a time. Beat in the egg yolk, remove from the heat and cool. Put ½ teaspoon of caramel in the bottom of each pastry case, then 1 teaspoon of chocolate ganache, and smooth the top. Whisk the heavy cream and confectioners' sugar until it forms soft peaks, and pipe swirls on top of the tarts.

NOW TRY THIS

chocolate orange french fancies
Prepare the basic recipe. Substitute a little orange marmalade for the caramel, and orange-flavored chocolate for the semisweet and milk chocolates. Cook and serve as before.

chocolate apricot french fancies
Prepare the basic recipe, substituting apricot jam for the caramel. Cook and serve as before.

chocolate peanut butter french fancies
Prepare the basic recipe, substituting peanut butter for the caramel. Cook and serve as before.

chocolate raspberry french fancies
Prepare the basic recipe, substituting raspberry jam for the caramel. Cook and serve as before.

chocolate whirls

These are pretty little cookies that taste as good as they look.

for the cookies

1 cup/8 oz. softened butter

½ cup/2 oz. confectioners' sugar

1 oz. bittersweet chocolate, melted

1 ¾ cups/8 oz. all-purpose flour

2 tbsp. Dutch process cocoa powder

3 tbsp. cornstarch

for the filling

4 tbsp. butter

1 ½ cups/6 oz. plus 1 tbsp. confectioners'
sugar, plus another 2 tbsp. for dusting

1 oz. bittersweet chocolate, melted

Makes 18

Pre-heat the oven to 350°F. To make the cookies, beat the butter and confectioners' sugar together, until light and fluffy. Stir in the chocolate. Sift the flour, cocoa powder, and cornstarch and stir into the creamed mixture.

Pipe the mixture, using a ¾-inch fluted nozzle, into 2-inch rosettes spaced 2 inches apart on a non-stick cookie sheet. Bake for 10–12 minutes until golden. Allow to firm up slightly before transferring them to a wire rack to cool.

To make the filling, beat the butter and confectioners' sugar together until light and fluffy and stir in the chocolate. Spread onto the bottom half of the cookies, and then sandwich together with the other halves. Dust with the 2 tablespoons of confectioners' sugar. You can store the filled cookies in an airtight container for 1–2 days and unfilled cookies for 5–7 days.

see photo on page 79

NOW TRY THIS

dipped chocolate whirls
Prepare the basic cookie dough and then half-dip the filled cookies in tempered bittersweet chocolate.

chocolate & ginger whirls
Prepare the basic dough, adding 1 teaspoon ground ginger to the flour and 2 tablespoons chopped candied ginger to the filling.

chocolate, cinnamon & raisin whirls
Prepare the basic cookie dough, adding 1 teaspoon ground cinnamon to the flour and 2 tablespoons raisins to the filling.

double chocolate whirls
Prepare the basic cookie dough, subsituting half the bittersweet chocolate for white chocolate.

mini peanut butter cups

Simple and fuss-free. These mini cups will be a hit at any cocktail party.

2 oz. milk chocolate, broken into pieces

2 tbsp. unsalted butter

3 tbsp. whipping cream

1 cup/9 oz. smooth peanut butter

2 tbsp. roasted peanuts (unsalted), chopped

Makes 12

Put 12 mini foil baking cups in a muffin pan.

Put the chocolate, butter, and cream in a double boiler and stir until smooth. Remove from the heat and set aside.

With damp hands, shape the peanut butter into 12 small flat circles. Push the peanut butter into the bottom of the cups. Pour the melted chocolate over the peanut butter, add a chopped peanut to the top, and refrigerate for at least 2 hours.

Store in an airtight container for up to 3 days.

see photo on page 79

NOW TRY THIS

mini marshmallow & peanut butter cups
Prepare the basic recipe. Add 1 cup/5 ½ ounces chopped large marshmallows to the melted chocolate mixture.

mini coconut & peanut butter cups
Prepare the basic recipe. Add 3 tablespoons sweetened coconut flakes to the melted chocolate.

mini jam & peanut butter cups
Prepare the basic recipe. Place a teaspoon of your favorite fruit jam into the bottom of the baking cups and top with the peanut butter and then the chocolate.

mini banana & peanut butter cups
Prepare the basic recipe. Add ½ mashed-up banana to the melted chocolate.

cherry pavlova bites

Crispy on the outside and gooey on the inside, these mini pavlovas just melt in the mouth.

6 egg whites, room temperature

1 ¼ cups/10 oz. superfine sugar

1 tsp. lemon juice

2 tsp. cornstarch

1 cup/8 oz. mascarpone

1 cup/8 oz. crème fraîche

1 tbsp. confectioners' sugar

1 tsp. vanilla extract

8 tbsp. good quality black cherry preserve

Makes 25

Pre-heat the oven to 250°F, and line two large cookie sheets with parchment. In a squeaky clean bowl, using an electric mixer, whisk the egg whites until they form soft peaks. Add the sugar a tablespoon at a time, whisking constantly, until all the sugar has been incorporated. Whisk in the lemon juice, and fold in the cornstarch.

Drop tablespoons of meringue onto the lined cookie sheets. Using the back of a teaspoon, form them into rounds, with a shallow indentation in the middle. Bake for 45–50 minutes, until the pavlovas are just firm to the touch, swapping the trays around halfway through cooking time. Turn the oven off, and leave the pavlovas to dry out in the oven, until they are cold.

In a large bowl, mix the mascarpone and crème fraîche together until well combined, and sweeten with confectioners' sugar. Stir in the vanilla extract. Put ½ teaspoon cherry preserve into the middle of each pavlova, followed by 1 tablespoon mascarpone, and top with 1 teaspoon cherry preserve. Swirl together with a cocktail stick. The unfilled pavlovas will keep for 2 days in an airtight container, but try not to fill until an hour or so before serving.

NOW TRY THIS

blueberry & lemon cream pavlova bites
Prepare the basic recipe, omitting the cherry preserve. Top the pavlovas with the mascarpone mix, add 1 teaspoon lemon curd and a few blueberries, and serve as before.

mont blanc pavlova bites
Prepare the basic recipe, omitting the cherry preserve, and substituting sweetened chestnut purée. Dust with confectioners' sugar to serve.

chocolate pavlova bites with caramel sauce
Prepare the basic recipe, adding 2 tablespoons sifted unsweetened cocoa powder to the beaten egg whites halfway through whisking. Omit the cherry preserve, top with the mascarpone mix, and drizzle each pavlova with caramel topping before serving, as before.

chocolate dipped mint creams

Dipping the mint creams in dark chocolate concentrates the flavor,
so that it bursts on your taste buds as you take a bite.

2 cups/8 oz. confectioners' sugar
1 egg white, lightly beaten
few drops peppermint extract
2 cups/12 oz. semisweet chocolate chips
Makes about 25

Line a large tray with parchment paper. Sift the confectioners' sugar into a large bowl, and blend with enough beaten egg white to form a stiff paste. Add a few drops of peppermint extract, to taste. Knead the paste lightly in the bowl, using your fingertips. Sprinkle a little confectioners' sugar onto a worktop, roll the paste out to ¼-inch thick, and stamp out 1-inch rounds with a plain cutter. Transfer the peppermint creams to the tray and let dry out for 24 hours. Turn them over occasionally, to dry both sides.

Melt the chocolate chips in a glass bowl over a pan of barely simmering water. Do not let the water touch the underside of the bowl. Using 2 forks, dip each peppermint cream into the chocolate. Lift them out, letting the excess drip off, and lay on a tray lined with fresh parchment paper, to dry and set. They will keep for up to 1 week in an airtight container. Do not refrigerate.

NOW TRY THIS

chocolate dipped coffee creams
Omit the peppermint extract. Substitute coffee extract, or ½ teaspoon instant coffee powder, and substitute milk chocolate chips for the semisweet chocolate chips.

chocolate dipped strawberry creams
Omit the peppermint extract. Substitute strawberry extract and a few drops of red food coloring to make the sugar paste pink, and substitute classic white chocolate chips for the semisweet chocolate chips.

chocolate dipped orange creams
Omit the peppermint extract. Substitute orange extract and a few drops of red and yellow food coloring to make the sugar paste orange, and substitute milk chocolate chips for the semisweet chocolate chips.

passion cake cookie sandwich

Filled with cream cheese, these delicious cookies taste like a little bite of heaven.

2 cups/9 oz. all-purpose flour
1 tsp. baking powder
1 tsp. baking soda
1 tsp. ground cinnamon
1 tsp. pumpkin pie spice
½ tsp. ground nutmeg
¼ tsp. salt
1 cup/8 oz. butter, room temperature
1 cup/8 oz. sugar
1 cup/8 oz. packed light brown sugar
2 eggs, room temperature
1 tsp. vanilla extract
2 cups/11 oz. rolled oats
1 ½ cups/8 oz. finely grated carrots
¼ cup/2 oz. finely chopped walnuts
1 cup/8 oz. cream cheese
Makes 40 cookie sandwiches

In a large bowl, sift the flour, baking powder, baking soda, cinnamon, pumpkin pie spice, nutmeg, and salt. Beat the butter with the sugars until light and fluffy. Add the eggs, one at a time, beating well between each one, then add the vanilla and beat until combined. Stir in the flour mixture, and mix in the oats, carrots, and walnuts. Chill in the refrigerator for 2 hours.

Line 2 cookie sheets with parchment. Pre-heat the oven to 350°F. Form the dough into about 40 small balls on the baking sheets, 2 inches apart, and bake for 12–15 minutes, until lightly browned and a little crisp on the edges. Cool on wire racks.

Once cooled completely, spread the cream cheese on half the cookies, and sandwich together with the remaining cookies. Store in an airtight container for 2–3 days in the refrigerator, and bring to room temperature before eating.

NOW TRY THIS

passion & ginger cookie sandwiches
Replace the pumpkin pie spice with 1 teaspoon ground ginger. Finely chop ⅓ cup/½ ounce candied ginger and add it to the filling.

passion & cardamom cookie sandwiches
Add the crushed seeds of 6 cardamom pods to the cookie dough mixture.

passion & coffee cake cookie sandwiches
Substitute the pumpkin pie spice with 2 teaspoons instant coffee powder, mixed with 1 tablespoon hot water, to the filling.

tropical passion cake cookie sandwiches
Replace the rolled oats with ⅓ cup/¾ ounce flaked coconut and the walnuts with chopped macadamia nuts.